YORK NOTES

C000293711

THE MERCHANT OF VENICE

WILLIAM SHAKESPEARE

NOTES BY MARTIN WALKER
REVISED BY EMMA PAGE

YORK PRESS
322 Old Brompton Road, London SW5 9JH

PEARSON EDUCATION LIMITED
Edinburgh Gate, Harlow,
Essex CM20 2JE, United Kingdom
Associated companies, branches and representatives throughout the world

First published 2018

10 9 8 7 6 5 4 3 2 1

ISBN 978–1–2922–3687–2

Illustrations by Sue Woollatt; and Alan Batley (page 64 only)
Phototypeset by DTP Media
Printed in Slovakia

Photo credits: Kotomiti Okuma/Shutterstock for page 8 / Rob Pitman/Shutterstock for page 9
left / Bioern Wylezich/Shutterstock for page 9 right / Kirimbay/Shutterstock for page 12 left /
Lynne Carpenter/Shutterstock for page 12 right / Denis Rozhnovsky/Shutterstock for page 12
bottom / Jordanhetrick/iStock for page 14 / Brian A Jackson/Shutterstock for page 20 / Mirelle/
Shutterstock for page 22 / Grafvision/Shutterstock for page 24 top / Ninell/Shutterstock for page
24 bottom / Tatiana Popova/Shutterstock for page 25 left / Eric Isselee/Shutterstock for page
25 right / Davydenko Yuliia/Shutterstock for page 26 / Bonzodog/Shutterstock for page 27 /
BrAt82/Shutterstock for page 30 / pavel891/Shutterstock for page 32 / STUDIO M/Shutterstock
for page 33 / Peshkova/Shutterstock for page 34 / Ilja Gerneralov/Shutterstock for page 35 /
Lynne Carpenter/Shutterstock for page 36 / izzet ugutmen/Shutterstock for page 37 / Chronicle/
Alamy Stock Photo for page 41 / Lebrecht Music and Arts Photo Library/Alamy for page 43 /
Denis Rozhnovsky/Shutterstock for page 45 bottom / Steve Collender/Shutterstock for page 46
/ Kate Aedon/Shutterstock for page 47 / outc/Shutterstock for page 48 / Tiggra/Shutterstock for
page 49 / AndreyCherkasov/Shutterstock for page 52 / PRISMA ARCHIVO/Alamy Stock Photo for
page 53 / samodelkin8/Shutterstock for page 54 left / photomaster/Shutterstock for page 54
middle / Anneka/Shutterstock for page 55 / Antonov Roman/Shutterstock for page 56 / Vvoronov/
Shutterstock for page 57 top / Netfalls Remy Musser/Shutterstock for page 57 bottom / Science
History Images/Alamy Stock Photo for page 58 middle / Watchara Ritjan/Shutterstock for page
58 bottom / Rsphotograph/Shutterstock for page 59 middle / Matteo Chinellato/Shutterstock for
page 59 bottom / InnaFelker/Shutterstock for page 60 / Lakeview Images/Shutterstock for page
62 / MorePixelsShutterstock/Shutterstock for page 63 / World History Archive/Alamy Stock Photo
for page 65 / NanayaViktoria/Shutterstock for page 66 / Denis Radovanovic/Shutterstock for page
67 / wk1003mike/Shutterstock for page 68 / Monkey Business Images/Shutterstock for page 77 /
Monkey Business Images/Shutterstock for page 79 / panitanphoto/Shutterstock for page 82

CONTENTS

PREPARING FOR ASSESSMENT

HOW WILL I BE ASSESSED ON MY WORK ON *THE MERCHANT OF VENICE*?

All exam boards are different, but whichever course you are following, your work will be examined through at least three of these four Assessment Objectives:

Assessment Objectives	Wording	Worth thinking about ...
AO1	Read, understand and respond to texts. Students should be able to: • maintain a critical style and develop an informed personal response • use textual references, including quotations, to support and illustrate interpretations.	• How well do I know what happens, what people say, do etc.? • What do *I* think about the key ideas in the play? • How can I support my viewpoint in a really convincing way? • What are the best quotations to use and when should I use them?
AO2	Analyse the language, form and structure used by a writer to create meanings and effects, using relevant subject terminology where appropriate.	• What specific things does the writer 'do'? What choices has Shakespeare made (Why this particular word, phrase or image here? Why does this event happen at this point?) • What effects do these choices create – amusement? tension? sympathy?
AO3 *	Show understanding of the relationships between texts and the contexts in which they were written.	• What can I learn about society from the play? (What does it tell me about attitudes to women and marriage, for example?) • What was society like in Shakespeare's time? Can I see it reflected in the text?
AO4 *	Use a range of vocabulary and sentence structures for clarity, purpose and effect, with accurate spelling and punctuation.	• How accurately and clearly do I write? • Are there small errors of grammar, spelling and punctuation I can get rid of?

* For *The Merchant of Venice*, AO3 is not examined by Eduqas; AO4 is not examined by Edexcel.

Look out for the Assessment Objective labels throughout your York Notes Study Guide – these will help to focus your study and revision!

The text used in this Study Guide is the Oxford School Shakespeare edition, 2010.

HOW TO USE YOUR YORK NOTES STUDY GUIDE

You are probably wondering what is the best and most efficient way to use your York Notes Study Guide on *The Merchant of Venice.* Here are three possibilities:

A **step-by-step** study and revision guide	A **'dip-in' support** when you need it	A **revision guide** after you have finished the text
Step 1: Read Part Two as you read the text, as a companion to help you study it. **Step 2:** When you need to, flip forward to Parts Three to Five to focus your learning. **Step 3:** Then, when you have finished, use Parts Six and Seven to hone your exam skills, revise and practise for the exam.	Perhaps you know the text quite well, but you want to check your understanding and practise your exam skills? Just look for the section you think you need most help with and go for it!	You might want to use the Notes after you have finished your study, using Parts Two to Five to check over what you have learned, and then working through Parts Six and Seven in the weeks leading up to your exam.

HOW WILL THE GUIDE HELP YOU STUDY AND REVISE?

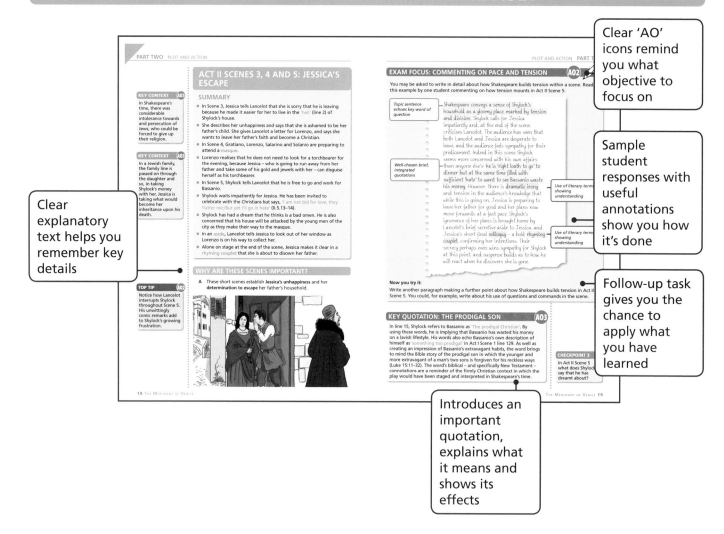

Clear explanatory text helps you remember key details

Clear 'AO' icons remind you what objective to focus on

Sample student responses with useful annotations show you how it's done

Follow-up task gives you the chance to apply what you have learned

Introduces an important quotation, explains what it means and shows its effects

Themes are explained clearly with bullet-points which give you ideas you might use in your essay responses

This section helps you tackle or explore challenging ideas or gives you a deeper insight into the writer's methods

Margin boxes draw your attention to important ideas or test your knowledge

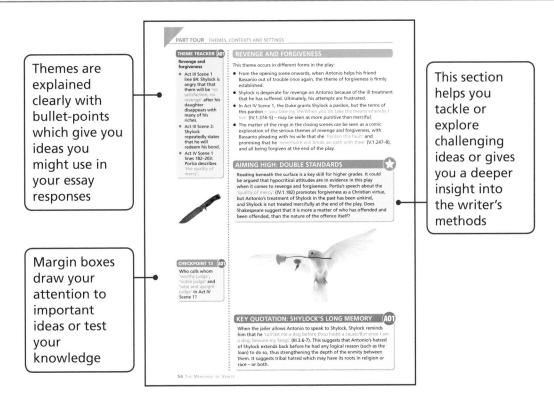

Parts Two to Five end with a **Progress and Revision check**:

Further substantial and 'open' tasks test your understanding

A set of quick questions tests your knowledge of the text

Self-evaluation – so you can keep a record of how you are getting on

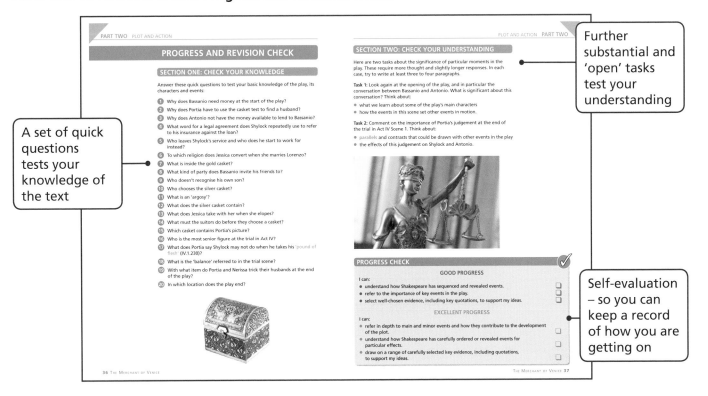

Don't forget Parts Six and Seven, with advice and practice on **improving your writing skills**:

- Focus on **difficult areas** such as **'context'** and **'inferences'**
- **Short snippets** of **other students' work** to show you how it's done (or not done!)
- Three annotated **sample responses** to a task **at different levels**, with **expert comments**, to help you judge your own level
- **Practice questions**
- **Answers** to the **Progress and Revision Checks** and **Checkpoint** margin boxes

Now it's up to you! Don't forget – there's even more help on our website with more sample answers, essay planners and even online tutorials. Go to www.yorknotes.com to find out more.

PLOT SUMMARY: WHAT HAPPENS IN *THE MERCHANT OF VENICE*?

ACT I: SHYLOCK'S BOND

TOP TIP A02

Think about what the audience learns in Act I about each character's backstory: about Bassanio's carelessness with money, for example, and about the enmity between Shylock and Antonio.

- At the start of the play, Antonio – a merchant of Venice – is depressed but doesn't know why he is 'so sad' (I.1.1). His friends Salarino and Solanio are attempting to rouse his spirits.
- The audience learns that all of Antonio's money is invested in his ships and merchandise, which are all still at sea.
- Bassanio, a close friend of Antonio, visits him. He has fallen in love with the beautiful heiress Portia and believes she returns his affections. He tells Antonio he wants to visit Belmont, where Portia lives, but does not want to arrive empty-handed.
- Bassanio has wasted his own fortune and a large sum of money that was loaned to him by Antonio. In spite of this, Antonio agrees to borrow money and give it to his friend.
- In Belmont, Portia waits nervously as various suitors try to win her hand. She cannot choose her own husband, but must marry the first man to pass a test set by her late father. Nerissa, Portia's lady-in-waiting and confidante, explains that the test uses 'three chests of gold, silver, and lead' (I.2.28–9) and that to win Portia's hand, a suitor must choose the right casket.

TOP TIP A03

The gold Venetian 'ducat' was an internationally recognised trade coin, in use from the thirteenth to the eighteenth century.

- Antonio and Bassanio go to Shylock, a Jewish moneylender and a bitter enemy of Antonio. Shylock agrees to lend the sum of 3,000 ducats if Antonio is to be bound by law to pay it back. Instead of charging interest, Shylock says that he will take a pound of Antonio's flesh if the loan is not repaid within three months. Antonio thinks this is kindness, but Bassanio is wary of Shylock's intentions. They arrange to visit a lawyer to formalise their arrangement.

ACT II: LOVING AND LEAVING

- In a comic scene, Shylock's servant Lancelot Gobbo leaves Shylock's service and goes to work for Bassanio.
- Portia's first suitor, the Prince of Morocco, arrives in Belmont to take the test.
- Jessica, Shylock's daughter, runs away with her Christian lover Lorenzo. They take Shylock's riches with them.
- The Prince of Morocco chooses the gold casket – the wrong choice.
- Bassanio sets sail for Belmont where he will attempt to win Portia's hand in marriage.
- The Prince of Arragon chooses the silver casket and also fails the test.

ACT III: ANTONIO IN TROUBLE

- The news that one of Antonio's ships has been lost at sea delights Shylock, who begins to think that he might now have his revenge upon Antonio for the terrible way in which the merchant has treated him over the years. He also learns of his daughter's elopement.

- Bassanio arrives in Belmont. It is clear that Portia desperately wants him to choose the correct casket, but cannot give him any help.
- Bassanio selects the lead casket and in it finds a portrait of Portia, showing he has chosen wisely.
- Meanwhile Bassanio's companion Gratiano has fallen in love with, proposed to and been accepted by Nerissa, Portia's maid.
- Before the couples can celebrate their marriages, a letter arrives from Venice saying that Antonio's ships have been lost and that Shylock is intent upon redeeming his bond.
- The men leave for Venice to try to pay Antonio's debt. They are wearing rings given to them by their wives.
- Shylock has Antonio arrested and taken to court.
- Portia asks her cousin, Doctor Bellario, to send her the costume of a lawyer and a letter recommending her to the Duke of Venice. She and Nerissa travel to Venice to help Antonio while Lorenzo and Jessica remain in Belmont with Lancelot.

ACT IV: THE TRIAL

- In court, no one is able to make Shylock change his mind about the bond. He even turns down an offer to pay him more than he is owed.
- Portia and Nerissa arrive, disguised as a lawyer and his clerk. Despite a powerful speech by Portia about 'the quality of mercy' (IV.1.182) Shylock continues to demand redemption of his bond. Portia plays along with Shylock, saying that he is entitled to take a pound of Antonio's flesh and encouraging him to insist that the absolute letter of the law be followed.
- As Shylock is about to take his knife to Antonio, Portia says that he must not spill so much as one drop of blood as blood is not mentioned in the bond: 'He shall have nothing but the penalty' (IV.1.320).
- Shylock loses the case and is punished for attempted murder by the confiscation of his wealth and by being forced to convert to Christianity.

ACT V: A FINAL TRICK

- Portia and Nerissa, still in disguise, insist upon being given the rings that Bassanio and Gratiano are wearing, as payment for saving their friend.
- Portia and Nerissa arrive back in Belmont just before their husbands and pretend that they have never been away. The wives ask to see that their husbands are still wearing the rings they were given. Of course, Portia and Nerissa actually have the rings.
- Bassanio and Gratiano are humiliated in front of Antonio, who has accompanied them, but all ends well when the wives admit to their joke. Jessica and Lorenzo are gathered with the others, but we see nothing of Shylock in this final act.

ACT I SCENE 1: BASSANIO'S PROBLEM

SUMMARY

- In Venice, Antonio seems despondent and troubled. His friends Salarino and Solanio wonder whether he is brooding on the fate of his various merchant ventures at sea. Antonio denies that this is the reason for his melancholy and Solanio suggests 'Why then, you are in love' (line 46).
- More friends – Lorenzo, Gratiano and Bassanio – arrive and together they try to raise their friend's spirits.
- Left alone, Bassanio explains to Antonio his problems regarding the rich and beautiful Portia. Antonio asks his friend to tell him about the lady to whom he has sworn 'a secret pilgrimage' (line 120).
- Bassanio describes how he has lived beyond his means and has wasted his fortune. Already in Antonio's debt, he asks Antonio to lend him more money so that he has the 'means/To hold a rival place' (lines 173–4) as one of Portia's suitors.
- Antonio is quite prepared to lend his friend the necessary money but all of his fortune is invested at sea, and he does not have such funds readily to hand. He suggests that they try to find out whether they can borrow the money in Venice in his name.

WHY IS THIS SECTION IMPORTANT?

A The audience is introduced to **Antonio**, the **'merchant of Venice'** who gives the play its title, and we learn about his business as a trader.

B We learn that **Bassanio and Antonio** are good **friends** and that Antonio is happy to help his friend despite his carelessness with money in the past.

C Another major plotline relating to **Portia's future husband** is also introduced.

KEY THEME: BASSANIO'S FINANCES A01

Bassanio faces a problem in attempting to woo Portia. She has attracted the interest of many wealthy men and if Bassanio does not act quickly he could lose out. As her other suitors are rich, Bassanio feels that he cannot arrive at Belmont without money. Not only has Bassanio squandered his own fortune, he has borrowed money from Antonio which he is unable to repay. Bassanio argues that if Antonio were prepared to lend him yet more money, he could use it to make his fortune and repay both debts to Antonio. In lines 140–52, Bassanio illustrates his argument using the image of a boy shooting an arrow in the same direction as one that has been lost. 'By adventuring both', he says, 'I oft found both' (lines 143–4). This image conveys Bassanio's youthful optimism and willingness to take a chance, perhaps anticipating his attitude to the casket test in Belmont.

KEY CHARACTER: ANTONIO (A01)

As a wealthy and well-known merchant, Antonio is a respectable member of Venetian society whose friendship is highly prized by Salarino, Solanio and the others. In particular, Bassanio – Antonio's 'kinsman' (line 57) – has found an unusually devoted patron in Antonio who is prepared to risk his life for his friend. The play begins with Antonio in a melancholy mood: 'In sooth I know not why I am so sad' (line 1). Some productions have interpreted Antonio's affection for Bassanio as the reason for his melancholy. Certainly, there is no mention in the play of Antonio wishing to find a wife and, later in the play, Antonio seems uneasy in Portia's presence.

KEY CONTEXT: MALE FRIENDSHIP (A03)

The close relationship Antonio has with Bassanio is often puzzling to modern audiences. In Shakespeare's time, men would have spent a great deal of time together without any women being around and this has certainly been the case with Antonio and Bassanio. Classical ideas about the spiritual bond of male friendship were also popular among many Elizabethans, and we need only look to Shakespeare's own sonnets for a famous example of this. It is possible to interpret Antonio's sadness as mourning the loss of a treasured male friend to married life.

KEY CONTEXT: CLASSICAL REFERENCES (A03)

Classical references such as the one about Jason and the Golden Fleece and the comparison of Portia to the wife of Brutus (Caesar's friend, assassin and 'the noblest Roman of them all') would have been understood by educated members of Shakespeare's audience. They establish that Bassanio is himself an educated man.

CHECKPOINT 1 (A01)

Where does Portia live?

ACT I SCENE 2: PORTIA AND HER SUITORS

SUMMARY

- In Belmont, Portia is complaining about her situation to her lady-in-waiting and friend Nerissa. She is reminded by Nerissa that she is actually very fortunate and should concentrate on keeping a level head. Portia says that it is easy to give advice but much more difficult to follow it.
- Nerissa describes the 'lottery … devised in these three chests of gold, silver, and lead' (lines 28–9) by Portia's father shortly before he died.
- Nerissa lists Portia's suitors and Portia makes fun of them. She dreads having to marry any one of these suitors.
- Nerissa reminds Portia of a young Venetian soldier who visited Belmont in her father's time. Portia remembers his name instantly 'Yes, yes, it was Bassanio! – as I think so was he called' (line 106), though she tries to play down her interest in him.
- Portia is ready to say more about Bassanio, but is prevented from doing so by the news that the Prince of Morocco is on his way.

WHY IS THIS SCENE IMPORTANT?

A We learn that Portia's father has stated in his will that **Portia cannot choose her** own **husband**, but instead she must marry whichever man chooses the correct **casket**.

B Portia is shown to be a **clever and witty woman**.

C Portia's interest in **Bassanio** hints at future plot developments.

KEY CONTEXT **A03**

In many of Shakespeare's plays, we are shown daughters who are torn between a father's wishes and their own desires. Examples include *Romeo and Juliet, A Midsummer Night's Dream, The Taming of the Shrew* and *Othello*. Consider also the parallel plot within this play involving Shylock and his daughter Jessica.

KEY LANGUAGE: PORTIA'S WIT   (A02)

When Nerissa asks her mistress if she has affection for any of her suitors, Portia launches into a savagely witty attack upon the men who have presented themselves so far:

- The Neapolitan Prince talks only of his horse.
- The County Palatine does nothing but frown.
- The French Lord does everything to excess. Portia says that he would drive her mad.
- Falconbridge, a young English baron, does not speak any of the languages that Portia speaks. He is good looking, but dressed in a mixture of styles from different countries.
- The Scottish lord has done nothing but fight with the Englishman.
- The German, the Duke of Saxony's nephew, is described as a drunkard.

Portia is a very witty character as is shown by her remarks about her suitors. In today's terms Portia's language would be considere racist as she uses stereotypical characteristics to attack them. In Elizabethan England, this would have been an acceptable way of creating humour.

KEY CONTEXT: IDEAS ABOUT MARRIAGE   (A03)

Portia is not able to choose her own husband. This was quite usual for women at this time as arranged marriages were normal for wealthy people and marriage was often carried out like a business transaction. Fortunately for Portia, her suitors until now have not agreed to the terms of her father's will and have recently left Belmont.

AIMING HIGH: VERSE AND PROSE

Unlike the previous scene, Act I Scene 2 is written entirely in prose. Elsewhere in the play, Portia and Nerissa will also use blank verse (unrhymed iambic pentameter), but the use of prose here indicates to audiences and readers that this is an informal, light-hearted and somewhat gossipy conversation between good friends. As you read the play, take note of where Shakespeare chooses blank verse or prose and consider the reasons behind each choice. Look for changes within a scene, for example in Act I Scene 1 where, in a brief section of prose (lines 114–18), Bassanio avoids the subject he wishes to talk to Antonio about before speaking more directly to him in blank verse in the lines that follow.

KEY CONTEXT   (A03)

Shakespeare draws on national and regional stereotypes to describe Portia's suitors. For example, Naples was famous for its horses and horsemanship, while Rhineland was celebrated for its white wine. Like the other suitors, the Neapolitan prince and the Duke of Saxony's nephew are caricatures for comic effect.

KEY CONTEXT   (A03)

Portia's latest suitor is black and is described as having 'the complexion of a devil' (lines 118–19). In Elizabethan times, smooth white skin was a sign of wealth and high status, and a common insult was to say that someone was sunburnt. People applied white lead to their faces to be fashionable, and many died of lead poisoning.

ACT I SCENE 3: A MEETING WITH SHYLOCK

SUMMARY

- Antonio and Bassanio visit Shylock so that Antonio can borrow money on behalf of Bassanio.
- The merchant asks Shylock to lend the money 'not/As to thy friends' (lines 127–8) but as if he were lending it to an enemy. Shylock recounts at length the ill treatment that he has received at the hands of Antonio.
- Shylock is interested to hear that Antonio will be responsible for repaying the debt.
- Shylock is well informed about Antonio's business, and is fully aware that all the merchant's money is invested at sea. He reflects upon the disasters that might befall a ship at sea before agreeing to Antonio and Bassanio's request.
- Antonio and Shylock arrange to go to a lawyer and sign a 'bond' (line 141) by which Antonio will be legally bound. If Antonio cannot repay the bond by the due date in three months' time, he will forfeit a pound of his own flesh.

TOP TIP (A02)

Antonio's ability to repay the loan is dependent upon his ships returning home safely.

Notice how Shakespeare echoes the first scene here. The conversations in Scene 1 about possible disasters at sea now become much more significant.

WHY IS THIS SCENE IMPORTANT?

A   This is the first appearance by **Shylock**, the play's most famous character.

B   Shylock agrees to **lend** Antonio **money** but asks for a **pound of flesh** as his **bond**.

C   The conversation is marked by **tension**, **resentment** and a **lack of trust**, in contrast to the supportive and close-knit relationships we have observed so far.

KEY CONTEXT (A03)

The practice of lending money at very high rates of interest is also known as usury and its practitioners as usurers. The word 'usance' (line 137) is used in this scene to mean 'interest'.

KEY CONTEXT: MONEYLENDING (A03)

Today people borrow money from banks and expect to be charged interest on the amounts borrowed. In Shakespeare's time, Christians were forbidden from lending out money in order to profit from it. Shylock is a focus for criticism because he lends money and charges interest but Jews were tolerated to an extent in Venetian society precisely because their religion allowed them to act like modern banks. This caused much resentment among Christians who found themselves indebted to Jews, and demonstrates the double standard that applied to Jews at the time. It is evident in this scene that Antonio does not like doing business with the Jews and that he is also very much against moneylending. He is forced to borrow money from Shylock and this angers him, especially when Shylock reminds Antonio that he had said that he would neither lend nor borrow money at interest.

EXAM FOCUS: DRAWING INFERENCES ABOUT CHARACTERS (A01)

You may be asked to write in detail about characters' relationships and shifting status within a scene. Read this example by one student commenting on the conversation between Antonio and Shylock in Act I Scene 3 and the conclusions we can draw from the language they use:

> Shylock offers Antonio a deal which appears to come out of friendship. He says that he will forgive and forget the insults and the attacks made upon him. Bassanio seems wary of Shylock's sudden kindness, but Antonio agrees to the Jew's terms without hesitation. He is unconcerned about forfeiting the bond as his ships are due home 'a month before the day' and there seems to be little doubt in Antonio's mind either in this scene or in Act I Scene I about the wisdom of letting Bassanio become one of his creditors again. However, the mood changes when Shylock describes the bond as a 'merry sport' – it is clear to all concerned that far more is at stake. Instead of remaining calm through this, Antonio loses his temper. Shakespeare shows the balance of power shifting between Antonio and Shylock in this scene with Shylock managing to achieve the upper hand.

Words like 'seems', 'appears' and 'suggests' demonstrate inference skills

Suggests words may carry deeper, darker meaning

Draws conclusions based on evidence presented

Now you try it:

Add a sentence explaining how Shakespeare presents Antonio as a more vulnerable figure by the end of this scene.

CHECKPOINT 1 (A01)

How much money does Antonio borrow on Bassanio's behalf?

KEY CONTEXT (A03)

The use of the word 'devil' (line 93) was both a common insult and an anti-Semitic one. Anti-Jewish slurs in this play include references to the devil and to animals.

ACT II SCENE 1: MOROCCO PREPARES TO TAKE THE TEST

SUMMARY

- Portia and the Prince of Morocco meet. The Prince is preparing to take the casket test.
- He is the latest in the line of Portia's suitors, and wishes to show his importance, his bravery and his wealth.
- Portia tells him that, if he fails the test, he must never 'speak to lady afterward/In way of marriage' (II.1.41–2). This is another condition of her father's will.
- The Prince is to go to the 'temple' (line 44) to take a binding oath before he attempts the test.

WHY IS THIS SCENE IMPORTANT?

A This short scene returns to Belmont and the **preparations** for the **first casket test**.

B Morocco agrees to the harsh terms of the test by taking a **formal oath**, reminding the audience perhaps of Shylock and Antonio's bond.

TOP TIP: WRITING ABOUT PREJUDICE (A03)

From the first line of this scene onwards, the Prince of Morocco – described in the stage directions as a 'tawny Moor' – seeks to overturn prejudice towards him and to be treated as a worthy suitor in every way: 'Mislike me not for my complexion' (line 1). As you study the play, find evidence of different kinds of prejudice and of the language used by characters to mock or insult characters who are perceived as different. What do your findings suggest about social attitudes to gender, class, race and religion in Elizabethan society?

AIMING HIGH: DRAWING BLOOD

Morocco challenges Portia to make an 'incision' (line 6) and to compare his blood to that of the fairest-skinned person in the world to 'prove whose blood is reddest, his or mine' (line 7). Red blood signified courage and virility, and this is one way of suggesting that Morocco is as noble and as eligible a suitor as a white man. You could compare and contrast Morocco's boast about his blood with Shylock's **rhetorical question** in the famous speech from Act III Scene 1: 'If you prick us, do we not bleed?' (III.1.57) and with Portia's ruling in Act IV Scene 1: 'Shed thou no blood' (IV.1.323). Consider the significance of the idea of 'blood' and its different meanings as you read on.

TOP TIP (A01)

Sometimes Morocco is played as a heroic man with great dignity. But there is ample scope in these lines for him to be played as a self-important fool. Explore both possibilities and see which one you prefer.

TOP TIP (A02)

Morocco expresses concern that because of 'blind Fortune' (line 36) he may lose out to an 'unworthier' (line 37) man. Keep track of references to 'risk', 'hazard' and 'fortune', both in this scene and as a **motif** throughout the play.

ACT II SCENE 2: LANCELOT AND HIS FATHER

SUMMARY

- In Venice, Lancelot Gobbo is on stage by himself and explains how he decided to leave Shylock's service.
- There then follows an absurd conversation between Lancelot and his father, Old Gobbo, in which the old man fails to recognise his son.
- Bassanio enters and is immediately approached by Old Gobbo, who asks for a job for his son. Bassanio agrees to take on Lancelot as his servant.
- Gratiano enters and tells Bassanio that he wishes to go with him to Belmont. Bassanio agrees on condition that Gratiano does not misbehave and so spoil his chance of courting Portia.

WHY IS THIS SCENE IMPORTANT?

A   **Lancelot**, who has just left Shylock's service, **amuses the audience** at his father's expense.

B   The **slapstick comedy** of this scene contrasts with the drama and rising tension of the previous scene.

C   Lancelot's move from Shylock's service to Bassanio's foreshadows **Jessica's elopement**, from Shylock's household (Jewish) to Bassanio's social circle (Christian).

KEY STRUCTURE: COMIC RELIEF   (A02)

This comic scene with Lancelot Gobbo occurs at the point when the audience want to see whether or not Morocco will choose the right casket. Comic scenes are often introduced to lighten the tone of the play and to keep the audience waiting. Tension is built up then relaxed in this manner throughout the play, as it would be too much to expect of an audience to remain in a state of tension for three hours.

KEY LANGUAGE: CLOWNING   (A02)

Lancelot Gobbo is this play's principal comic figure. This scene begins with Lancelot alone on stage explaining how, like a character in a medieval morality play, he was torn between doing right and wrong – between his 'conscience', and the 'fiend' – in his decision about leaving Shylock's service. Shakespeare creates much comedy in Lancelot's long-winded description of this dilemma: '"Budge!" says the fiend. "Budge not!" says my conscience.' (lines 17–18)

There is visual humour in the scene too – Gobbo mistakes his kneeling son's hair for a long beard in lines 87–9 – but much of the comedy of the scene derives from errors in the two men's use of words, or malapropisms. Examples in this scene include 'the devil incarnation' (instead of incarnate) in line 24, and 'the suit is impertinent' (instead of pertinent) in line 127. Can you find further examples?

> **TOP TIP**   (A02)
>
> Shakespeare often uses mistaken identity in his plays. Sometimes it results in tragedy; sometimes, as in this scene, it is used for comic effect. Compare this scene with Jessica's disguise as a page boy and with Shakespeare's use of disguise in Acts IV and V in which Portia and Nerissa dress as Balthazar and his clerk.

> **TOP TIP**   (A01)
>
> Look out for variations of spelling across different editions of the play, particularly where names are concerned. For example, Lancelot is commonly spelled 'Launcelot' and some editions print Salarino's name as 'Salerio'.

ACT II SCENES 3, 4 AND 5: JESSICA'S ESCAPE

SUMMARY

- In Scene 3, Jessica tells Lancelot that she is sorry that he is leaving because he made it easier for her to live in the 'hell' (line 2) of Shylock's house.
- She describes her unhappiness and says that she is ashamed to be her father's child. She gives Lancelot a letter for Lorenzo, and says she wants to leave her father's faith and become a Christian.
- In Scene 4, Gratiano, Lorenzo, Salarino and Solanio are preparing to attend a masque.
- Lorenzo realises that he does not need to look for a torchbearer for the evening, because Jessica – who is going to run away from her father and take some of his gold and jewels with her – can disguise herself as his torchbearer.
- In Scene 5, Shylock tells Lancelot that he is free to go and work for Bassanio.
- Shylock waits impatiently for Jessica. He has been invited to celebrate with the Christians but says, 'I am not bid for love, they flatter me;/But yet I'll go in hate' (II.5.13–14).
- Shylock has had a dream that he thinks is a bad omen. He is also concerned that his house will be attacked by the young men of the city as they make their way to the masque.
- In an aside, Lancelot tells Jessica to look out of her window as Lorenzo is on his way to collect her.
- Alone on stage at the end of the scene, Jessica makes it clear in a rhyming couplet that she is about to disown her father.

WHY ARE THESE SCENES IMPORTANT?

A These short scenes establish **Jessica's unhappiness** and her **determination to escape** her father's household.

KEY CONTEXT (A03)

In Shakespeare's time, there was considerable intolerance towards and persecution of Jews, who could be forced to give up their religion.

KEY CONTEXT (A03)

In a Jewish family, the family line is passed on through the daughter and so, in taking Shylock's money with her, Jessica is taking what would become her inheritance upon his death.

TOP TIP (A02)

Notice how Lancelot interrupts Shylock throughout Scene 5. His unwittingly comic remarks add to Shylock's growing frustration.

EXAM FOCUS: COMMENTING ON PACE AND TENSION (A02)

You may be asked to write in detail about how Shakespeare builds tension within a scene. Read this example by one student commenting on how tension mounts in Act II Scene 5:

> **Topic sentence echoes key word of question**

Shakespeare conveys a sense of Shylock's household as a gloomy place, marked by tension and division. Shylock calls for Jessica impatiently and, at the end of the scene, criticises Lancelot. The audience has seen that both Lancelot and Jessica are desperate to leave, and the audience feels sympathy for their predicament. Indeed in this scene Shylock seems more concerned with his own affairs than anyone else's:

> **Well-chosen brief, integrated quotations**

he is 'right loath to go' to dinner but at the same time filled with sufficient 'hate' to want to see Bassanio waste his money. However, there is dramatic irony and tension in the audience's knowledge that while this is going on, Jessica is preparing to leave her father for good and her plans now move forwards at a fast pace. Shylock's ignorance of her plans is brought home by Lancelot's brief secretive aside to Jessica, and Jessica's short final soliloquy – a bold rhyming couplet, confirming her intentions. Their secrecy perhaps even wins sympathy for Shylock at this point, and suspense builds as to how he will react when he discovers she is gone.

> **Use of literary terms showing understanding**

> **Use of literary terms showing understanding**

Now you try it:

Write another paragraph making a further point about how Shakespeare builds tension in Act II Scene 5. You could, for example, write about his use of questions and commands in the scene.

KEY QUOTATION: THE PRODIGAL SON (A03)

In line 15, Shylock refers to Bassanio as 'The prodigal Christian'. By using these words, he is implying that Bassanio has wasted his money on a lavish lifestyle. His words also echo Bassanio's own description of himself as 'something too prodigal' in Act I Scene 1 line 129. As well as creating an impression of Bassanio's extravagant habits, the word brings to mind the Bible story of the prodigal son in which the younger and more extravagant of a man's two sons is forgiven for his reckless ways (Luke 15:11–32). The word's biblical – and specifically New Testament – connotations are a reminder of the firmly Christian context in which the play would have been staged and interpreted in Shakespeare's time.

> **CHECKPOINT 3 (A01)**
>
> In Act II Scene 5 what does Shylock say that he has dreamt about?

ACT II SCENE 6: LOVERS AND SUITORS

SUMMARY

- In Venice, outside Shylock's house, the young men are on their way to the **masque**. Gratiano and Salarino are waiting for Lorenzo who is late. Gratiano says that people in love are usually far too early: 'lovers ever run before the clock' (line 5) and speaks at some length about how 'All things that are/Are with more spirit chased than enjoy'd.' (line 14)
- Jessica appears on the balcony of her father's house, dressed as a page boy. She throws a casket of money and jewels to Lorenzo.
- Lorenzo and Jessica leave for the masque with the others.
- Antonio hears that the masque has been cancelled as the wind has changed direction and Bassanio can now set sail for Belmont.

WHY IS THIS SCENE IMPORTANT?

- **A** Jessica and Lorenzo **elope** together.
- **B** Bassanio will **set sail for Belmont** immediately.
- **C** The mention of the wind reminds the audience of **Antonio's ships** on whose safe return his life may depend.

KEY SETTINGS: VENICE AND BELMONT A03

Belmont is some distance away from Venice. This means that it takes time for information – and the characters – to travel from one location to another. This allows possibilities for messages arriving late and characters missing one another as they travel between the two. Shakespeare makes use of this on several occasions in the play. The first instance is here with the ship's departure being delayed just long enough for the audience to become worried about the Prince of Morocco's choice in the casket test.

KEY CONTEXT: THE ELIZABETHAN STAGE A03

The 'penthouse' (line 1) under which the masquers stand is a reminder to modern audiences that an Elizabethan theatre would have had a gallery above the stage. When Jessica enters and then exits 'above', this shows that she briefly appears on the gallery (to indicate that she is looking down from a window in Shylock's house). Later in the scene she appears on, and then exits with Lorenzo from, the main stage, indicating that she has made her escape.

ACT II SCENE 7: MOROCCO TAKES THE TEST

SUMMARY

- In Belmont, the Prince of Morocco has to choose between the caskets of gold, silver and lead. Portia shows the Prince of Morocco to the caskets and asks him to make his choice.

- Morocco reads the inscription on each of the three caskets. On the gold casket it says 'Who chooseth me, shall gain what many men desire' (line 5) and on the silver casket it says 'Who chooseth me, shall get as much as he deserves' (line 7). On the lead casket it says 'Who chooseth me, must give and hazard all he hath' (line 16).

- Portia tells him that one of the caskets contains her picture. If he chooses the right one then she will be his.

- Morocco takes a very long time to decide. He dismisses the lead casket as he thinks that lead is not worth risking everything for and the silver casket because it does not seem grand enough to signify Portia. He eventually settles upon the gold casket because it is the most precious.

- His choice is incorrect and instead of Portia's picture, he finds a skull and a scroll that begins 'All that glisters is not gold' (line 65). Severely disappointed, he leaves with his followers. Portia makes it clear that she is pleased about this outcome with her remark: 'A gentle riddance!' (line 78).

WHY IS THIS SCENE IMPORTANT?

A   The **Prince of Morocco fails** in his attempt to win Portia's hand in marriage.

B   The audience learns more about the **caskets** and how the casket test works.

C   **Suspense** builds as to which suitor will be successful.

KEY LANGUAGE: THE INSCRIPTIONS (A02)

The inscriptions on the caskets speak to the suitors in riddles and give Morocco much to think about. On the scroll inside the gold casket is a nine-line poem, pointing out that Morocco has chosen foolishly. The poem begins with the memorable line about appearances being deceiving: 'All that glisters is not gold' (line 65) which, like many of Shakespeare's phrases, has become familiar as a popular saying. The line uses alliteration and the nine lines of the poem all rhyme with each other: 'gold'/'told'/'sold'/'behold', etc. Combined with the use of tetrameter and the way that most lines in the poem begin with a stressed syllable, the taunting message on the scroll could not be more direct or more chilling. Where Morocco had hoped to find love, he finds a 'memento mori' – a reminder of death.

KEY CONTEXT (A03)

The four main elements of the plot of *The Merchant of Venice* were well-known stories in 1598 when the play was first written (see 'The play's sources', page 58). The episode of the caskets originated in medieval tales, and other elements were Italian stories of the sixteenth century. Shakespeare borrowed from these various sources, changing them to suit his own dramatic purposes.

TOP TIP (A01)

Consider different ways in which the casket scenes have been and could be staged to create comedy, sympathy, tension, etc. A key question is whether Portia secretly knows which casket is which and whether it is possible that she has been so devious as to 'rig' the outcome.

ACT II SCENE 8: BAD NEWS FOR SHYLOCK AND ANTONIO

SUMMARY

- Salarino and Solanio are discussing the departure of Bassanio's ship. Shylock had attempted to have the ship searched to find Lorenzo and Jessica. The ship had already sailed, but there have been reports that the pair have been seen together in a gondola.
- We learn that Shylock is beside himself with a mixture of anger and grief at Jessica's disappearance with his money.
- News has reached Venice that 'A vessel of our country richly fraught' (line 31) has sunk in the English Channel. Solanio hopes that it is not one of Antonio's ships.
- Salarino reports that Antonio, despite being in debt to Shylock, has told Bassanio not to rush his wooing of Portia and so reduce his chances of success.
- Salarino and Solanio set off to look for Antonio.

WHY IS THIS SCENE IMPORTANT?

A Though neither of them makes an appearance in this scene, the audience hears reports of both **Shylock and Antonio**.

B There is a chance that the **shipwrecked vessel** is one of Antonio's.

C We are reminded of Antonio's **loyalty and affection** for Bassanio.

KEY CHARACTERS: MINOR CHARACTERS (A02)

Salarino and Solanio, along with Lancelot, are used by Shakespeare to fill in gaps in the story and to update the audience on recent events. This can allow the plot to move along more swiftly. They also highlight the attitudes of ordinary people of the day, in this case towards Jews. Note the attitude of Solanio and Salarino towards Shylock. They describe him as a 'villain' (line 4) and a 'dog' (line 14). They seem to view him as a figure of fun and are pleased that he has suffered.

KEY QUOTATION: SHYLOCK'S CONFUSION (A02)

Solanio tells us that Shylock has been heard to cry 'My daughter! O my ducats! O my daughter!' (line 15) which suggests that he does not know whether it is the loss of his daughter or his money that upsets him more. Solanio remarks that he 'never heard a passion so confus'd' (line 12); however, it is important to remember that this is a report of Shylock's reaction and one that mocks and belittles him, perhaps unfairly.

KEY CONTEXT (A03)

Shakespeare's references to the 'Rialto' (I.3.17) and, in this scene, 'gondola' (line 8) are reminders of the play's Venetian setting.

KEY CONTEXT (A03)

This scene is one of several places in the play where the influence of fellow playwright Christopher Marlowe's *The Jew of Malta* (first performed in 1592) is clear. Marlowe's main character Barabas also has a daughter (Abigail) who converts to Christianity and, like Shylock, his love for his child and his love for his money are hard to separate: 'O my girl/My gold, my fortune, my felicity'.

ACT II SCENE 9: THE PRINCE OF ARRAGON

SUMMARY

- The Prince of Arragon has arrived to take the test of the caskets. Portia shows them to him and explains the conditions attached: he must never reveal to anyone the casket which he chose; if he chooses wrongly he must leave at once, and must never ask a woman to marry him.

- Arragon does a great deal of deliberating about his choice of casket. He reasons that the message on the gold casket makes it too popular for him to choose. He finally settles upon the silver one as he feels that he deserves Portia.

- When he opens the casket he finds a 'portrait of a blinking idiot' (line 53), and an accompanying nine-line rhyme telling him that he is a fool and ending with 'So be gone, you are sped' (line 71).

- Arragon leaves and a messenger enters to say that another lord has arrived. The new arrival is Venetian and his companion is described as 'So likely an ambassador of love' (line 91).

WHY IS THIS SCENE IMPORTANT?

A   A **second suitor** takes the casket test and **fails**.
B   There is eager **anticipation** as a Venetian lord bearing 'Gifts of rich value' (line 90) approaches Belmont.
C   **Bassanio's arrival** is announced by a messenger who is full of praise for the new suitor's companion.

ACT III SCENE 1: TROUBLE AND DESPAIR

SUMMARY

- Salarino tells Solanio of the rumour that Antonio has lost a ship, run aground on 'the Goodwins' (line 4).
- Shylock enters and immediately confronts the two men who mock him mercilessly. He is sure that they knew that his daughter was planning to run away.
- Shylock tells of all the times that Antonio has insulted him and his friends. He is intent upon revenge should Antonio fail to repay the money he has borrowed for Bassanio.
- A servant brings a message that Antonio is looking for Salarino and Solanio.
- Shylock's friend Tubal, a wealthy Jew, arrives to tell Shylock what he knows about Jessica's movements since she ran away. Shylock's sadness at the loss of his daughter is mixed with despair at the loss of his wealth. He even says that he wishes Jessica were dead at his feet along with the jewels she has stolen.
- Tubal tells Shylock that he has heard that Antonio has lost a ship returning from Tripoli in North Africa. Shylock is overjoyed at the news and the power this gives him over Antonio.

KEY CONTEXT (A03)
Ships frequently ran into difficulty on Goodwin Sands in the English Channel, not far from the Deal coast in Kent.

WHY IS THIS SCENE IMPORTANT?

A It seems that Antonio has suffered **losses at sea**.
B **Shylock is mocked** by the Christians, and hears of his **humiliation** at the hands of his daughter who has spent much of his wealth.
C This increases Shylock's **hatred of Christians** and his **desire for revenge** on Antonio grows.

KEY LANGUAGE: CRUEL WORDPLAY

In the early part of this scene, Shylock accuses Salarino and Solanio of prior knowledge of his daughter's flight. In return, Salarino teases Shylock by saying he knew the tailor that made her wings and Solanio says that Shylock should have known that a bird leaves its nest once its feathers have grown. Solanio uses the word 'dam' (line 28) meaning mother bird and, in his response, Shylock uses a **pun** saying that Jessica 'is damned for it' (line 29).

When Shylock refers to Jessica as his flesh and blood, Salarino insults him by saying that the difference between the flesh and blood of this father and daughter is like that 'between jet and ivory … between red wine and Rhenish' (white wine, lines 35–6). **Motifs** of flesh and blood recur in this scene when Salarino suggests Shylock will not really take Antonio's 'flesh. What's that good for? (lines 45–6), and in Shylock's speech: 'If you prick us, do we not bleed?' (line 57).

KEY CONTEXT: RELIGIOUS ARGUMENTS (A03)

In this scene, Shylock delivers one of Shakespeare's most famous speeches, opening with 'Hath not a Jew eyes?' (line 52). Shylock says that a Jew is a man like any other, with the same feelings. He argues that Christians take revenge when they are wronged, so why shouldn't a Jew do the same? It follows, he argues, that the Christian – Antonio – will be treated as he treats others. Shylock's speech (lines 47–65) contains many ideas taken straight from the teachings of the Christian Church. In this way, Shylock is using the Christians' own arguments against them.

KEY CHARACTER: SHYLOCK (A01)

Much of Shylock's speech is in prose. This is unusual for major speeches and makes him appear more human and more vulnerable, and therefore may invite the audience's sympathy. His despair about his losses may also begin to seem less mercenary and more sentimental as he discovers that Jessica has traded a valuable turquoise ring that once belonged to Leah (presumably Shylock's wife and Jessica's mother) – for nothing more than a monkey. However, elsewhere in this scene, the close repetition of the phrase 'let him look to his bond' (lines 41–2), and Shylock's determination to exact his revenge, make him sound calculating and menacing. This scene may confirm him in the audience's mind as a cruelly unforgiving and even villainous character.

CHECKPOINT 5 (A01)

From where does Tubal arrive, bringing news of both Jessica and Antonio?

TOP TIP (A01)

Consider how Shylock reacts to each piece of news about his daughter's extravagance. How sympathetically might audiences view Jessica's spending?

TOP TIP: WRITING ABOUT MINOR CHARACTERS (A02)

Once again, consider the dramatic function of the more minor characters Salarino and Solanio in the play. Notice how they report to the audience incidents that have taken place off-stage, just as they did in Act II Scene 8. Their language also reflects the anti-Semitic attitudes that would have been commonly held by audiences at the time.

TOP TIP (A02)

Notice how Shakespeare keeps Portia and the audience waiting while the music plays and Bassanio decides, even though the outcome is not really in doubt. This is to develop tension. Notice also that the rhyming words at the end of the lines of the song – 'bred', 'head', 'nourished' – all point towards 'lead' as the correct answer!

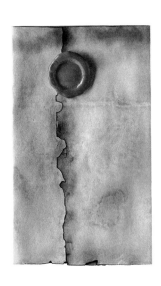

ACT III SCENE 2: BASSANIO AND THE CASKETS

SUMMARY

- Portia wants Bassanio to wait before making the choice of the caskets but he wishes to take the test immediately.
- Although Portia would like to teach Bassanio 'How to choose right' (line 11), she cannot because she is bound by the terms of her father's will.
- There is then some music while Bassanio examines the caskets. He reflects on the theme of appearance and reality, and the need to look beyond 'fair ornament' (line 80).
- Bassanio rejects the caskets of gold and silver and chooses the lead casket. Inside he finds a portrait of Portia – 'Fair Portia's counterfeit!' (line 115) – showing he is successful. The couple are ecstatically happy and Portia gives Bassanio a ring as a token of her love.
- Gratiano announces that he and Nerissa have fallen in love and wish to be married.
- Lorenzo, Jessica and Salerio – a messenger from Venice – enter. Bassanio is given a letter from Antonio saying that all the merchant's ventures have failed due to disaster at sea. Salerio says that Shylock is determined to have his pound of flesh; no one in Venice has been able to persuade him to change his mind.
- Portia offers to give Shylock much more money than he is owed and asks Bassanio to take it to Venice.

WHY IS THIS SCENE IMPORTANT?

A Bassanio's **success** in the **casket test** is a joyful moment in the play.
B The mood changes when Bassanio receives **bad news about Antonio**.

KEY THEME: LOVE AND MARRIAGE (A01)

In this scene, Shakespeare mixes the language of courtly love (with its idealised notions of beauty) with a more realistic language of love. For example, in lines 53–62 Portia compares her situation to that of Hesione, a beautiful young woman of Troy, who was to be sacrificed to a sea monster, and whom Hercules rescued. However, she later tells Bassanio that she is really just an ordinary woman – 'unlesson'd, unschool'd, unpractis'd' (line 159). She is not the fantastic 'thrice-fair lady' (line 146) that he compares to the precious commodities 'sugar' (line 119) and gold (line 122). This also links to the theme of appearance and reality.

TOP TIP: WRITING ABOUT RHYME (A02)

Portia's speech, lines 40–62, ends in a rhyming couplet. This is unusual within a scene and suggests that something important is to about to occur. What happens next?

KEY CONTEXT: THE PRICE OF MARRIAGE (A03)

In Renaissance times, a marriage was a financial and material transaction as well as a personal and romantic one. While the couple's reactions show their love for each other, they also reflect attitudes of the day towards the status of men and women in marriage. Portia says that everything she has, including herself, now belongs to Bassanio whom she calls 'her lord, her governor, her king' (line 165). To a modern audience, these words may jar, given that Portia has shown herself to be a clever and capable heroine.

AIMING HIGH: APPEARANCE AND REALITY

The idea of looking beyond appearances is demonstrated as Bassanio muses on which casket he should open. In the first line of his speech (lines 73–107), he comments 'So may the outward shows be least themselves:/The world is still deceiv'd with ornament' (lines 73–4). In the lines that follow, he makes a number of perceptive points:

- A guilty person might plead their innocence eloquently (lines 75–7).
- Evil deeds are often explained away by referring to a passage of scripture (lines 77–80).
- Cowards may grow beards to show that they are brave, but their livers are still white (lines 83–8).
- Cosmetics and wigs and other adornments can be bought by the kilo but the person who uses them the most is likely to be the least beautiful and least worthy (lines 88–101).

In Bassanio's view, lead does not make false promises, unlike 'gaudy gold' (line 101). His thoughts provide an interesting commentary on the social, religious and economic forces that govern characters' actions in the play. What other examples of this theme can you find in the play and what do they tell us about the lives of the characters?

CHECKPOINT 6 (A01)

Complete this quotation from the start of Act III Scene 2: 'I pray you tarry, pause a day or two/ Before you _____'.

KEY CONTEXT (A03)

The 'rack' (line 25) was an instrument of torture, used to make people confess to treason. A white liver (line 86) was thought to indicate cowardice.

ACT III SCENE 3: ANTONIO IS IMPRISONED

SUMMARY

- On a Venetian street. Shylock instructs a jailer to imprison Antonio. Antonio tries to get Shylock to listen to him but the Jew is set upon revenge and will not listen to anyone.
- Antonio realises that Shylock wishes to kill him, but he thinks that this is because he has often released people from their debts to Shylock.
- Antonio's thoughts once again turn to Bassanio.

TOP TIP

As in Act III Scene 1, Shylock repeatedly mentions 'my bond' (lines 4–17). What do you think this repetition might suggest about Shylock's state of mind?

WHY IS THIS SCENE IMPORTANT?

A   Shylock is one step closer to securing his **'pound of flesh'** from Antonio.

B   **Antonio** is melancholy but seems **resigned to his fate**.

AIMING HIGH: THE LAW, TRADE AND VENICE

Don't forget to consider the importance of Venice as a location for the play and as a key element in the plot. The Duke of Venice is the most powerful character in the play, but not even he can break the terms of the bond. As a merchant, Antonio understands that Venice would lose its reputation as an honest trading centre if the Duke broke his own laws.

ACT III SCENES 4 AND 5: PORTIA'S PLAN

SUMMARY

- In Scene 4, Lorenzo praises Portia's generosity in offering to pay back the money that Antonio owes, and says she would be even prouder of her offer if she knew what a true gentleman Antonio was. Portia replies that she is sure Antonio must be very like Bassanio as the two are such close friends.

- She entrusts her house to Lorenzo (and Jessica) and says that she and Nerissa will live in a monastery until their husbands return.

- Portia sends her servant Balthazar to Padua with a note for her cousin Doctor Bellario, a lawyer. Balthazar is to take whatever documents and clothing he is given to Venice as quickly as he can.

- Portia tells Nerissa that they will see their husbands soon as they are to go to Venice dressed as men.

- In Scene 5, Lancelot teases Jessica, saying that he fears she is damned because she is the daughter of a Jew. She announces that she will be 'saved' (line 16) by her husband Lorenzo because he has made her a Christian.

- The scene ends with more foolery from Lancelot who has accompanied his new master Bassanio to Belmont, and with a brief conversation between the newlyweds Lorenzo and Jessica.

TOP TIP (A02)

There are no significant plot developments in Act III Scene 5. This scene is another example of Shakespeare using a comic interlude to lighten the mood of the play. In practical terms, the scene also allows the actors playing Portia and Nerissa to dress for the next scene.

TOP TIP (A01)

Notice how there is hardly any conversation between Portia and Jessica. This is in contrast to the sudden closeness formed between Portia and Bassanio and Nerissa and Gratiano. Think about why this might this be.

WHY IS THIS SCENE IMPORTANT?

A   The audience learns of **Portia's plan** to help Antonio.
B   The play's two settings – **Venice and Belmont** – are now much more firmly interconnected as characters move between them.
C   Antonio's trial approaches – but there is **comedy** to lighten the mood.

AIMING HIGH: WRITING ABOUT MEN AND WOMEN

At the end of Scene 4, as she explains to Nerissa that the two of them will dress up as men, Portia gives an amusing account of the typical behaviour of young men. On two occasions (lines 60–2 and lines 79–80), Portia makes sexually explicit jokes to Nerissa. This shows her to be a little more worldly-wise than she might at first seem, though Shakespeare also makes it very clear that she is a virtuous and devoted wife and that all her actions are motivated by her love for her husband, and her generosity towards his friends. The scene builds anticipation for Portia and Nerissa's appearance dressed as men in the next scene, as they set out to help Antonio in his hour of need. The audience is being given advance warning of the two women's plans to dress as a lawyer and his clerk but, as we will see, the other characters will be entirely fooled by their disguises in Act IV Scene 1.

ACT IV SCENE 1: THE TRIAL

SUMMARY

- The Duke of Venice expresses his sympathy for Antonio, but Antonio says there is nothing more the Duke can do if Shylock remains determined. Shylock is summoned and the Duke pleads with him to show mercy.

- Shylock states that he will take the 'pound of flesh' (line 230) that is due to him. He points out that if the Duke denies him his legal rights, this would make the city-state's independence worthless. Despite Bassanio's attempts to reason with Shylock, he will not change his mind.

- Antonio resigns himself to his fate. Bassanio offers the Jew twice the money he is owed but Shylock says he would not accept even six times the debt.

- Nerissa enters, disguised as a lawyer's clerk and gives the Duke a letter from Doctor Bellario.

- Portia enters, disguised as Doctor Balthazar, and appeals to Shylock for mercy. Shylock insists on the law being upheld, even after Portia points out that he has been offered three times the money owed him. Portia asks for a surgeon to be brought to stop Antonio from bleeding to death but Shylock will not allow this as it is not stated in the terms of the bond.

- Antonio prepares to die and Bassanio says that even though he has just married, he would gladly give himself, his wife and all the world to save Antonio. Portia adds that his wife would not thank him for making such an offer and Gratiano announces that he wishes his wife were dead so that she could plead with God to make Shylock change his mind.

- Shylock is about to cut into Antonio's flesh when Portia stops him. She points out that the bond allows him to take a 'pound of flesh' (line 230), but does not mention shedding one drop of blood. Antonio is saved and Shylock is left with only 'justice and his bond' (line 337) and not even his original payment.

- It is agreed that Antonio will take only half of Shylock's money in trust until Shylock's death when it will be passed on to Lorenzo. Antonio agrees to this on condition that Shylock converts to Christianity and promises the rest of his money to Lorenzo and Jessica in his will.

- Portia says she will take no money for her services, but insists that Bassanio should give her his ring, which he does.

WHY IS THIS SCENE IMPORTANT?

A It is the **dramatic climax** of the play, full of tension and, finally, resolution.

B It brings together the key themes of **justice**, **revenge** and **financial dealings**.

C **Portia's** clever intervention in the trial is further proof of her **intelligence**.

KEY STRUCTURE: CLIMAX AND REVERSAL (A02)

Shakespeare builds tension throughout this pivotal scene. Shylock firmly stands his ground and voices his admiration for the young lawyer who appears to be supporting his case. For example, when Portia says that Shylock is quite entitled under the law to cut off a pound of Antonio's flesh, Shylock says that the lawyer is as wise as Daniel, a figure known for his youth as well as his powers of judgement, in the Hebrew Bible. In a demonstration of legal skill, Portia exposes how merciless Shylock is in his pursuit of what he considers to be a just revenge, only to turn the tables on him as the scene reaches a tense climax.

Portia then pursues Shylock by insisting that can take only what it is due to him in the bond. He cannot now decide to take the money (the 'principal' in line 334) that he earlier refused. She goes further by saying that in attempting to kill a Christian, Shylock has broken the laws of Venice. Under these laws, the victim (Antonio) is due half of Shylock's wealth and the state of Venice the other half. In addition, Shylock's life is in the hands of the Duke. His life is spared, but the sudden reversal in the fortunes of the moneylender and the merchant is complete.

AIMING HIGH: JUSTICE IN ENGLAND AND VENICE

Shakespeare's portrayal of the laws of Venice is in fact an adaptation of the laws of England in the sixteenth century. Such laws allowed non-Christians very few rights and were aimed at protecting the wealthy. Shylock is quite entitled to take a 'pound of flesh' (line 230) but he is so enraged that he seems more motivated by revenge than justice. It could also be argued that the same is true of Portia, Antonio and the others, once Antonio is saved. Shylock is shown no mercy and ends the play silenced, humiliated and alone. The play – and this scene of the play in particular – raises questions about the concept of justice and the laws and legal systems that are designed to achieve justice in practice. In this play, what values are upheld by the Venetian system of law and who is protected by the law?

KEY CONTEXT (A03)

Antonio has been affected by the thinking of the time in which he lived. Shakespeare's audience would not have seen Antonio's actions as being unjust; they would have expected to see the Jew being punished.

KEY CONTEXT (A03)

The laws regarding an 'alien' (line 347) plotting the murder of a citizen apply to Shylock because he is Jewish. A Christian would not receive such harsh treatment.

KEY LANGUAGE: PORTIA'S MERCY   (A02)

Portia uses the words 'mercy' and 'merciful' several times in this scene and her appeal for mercy in lines 182–203 is moving and extremely effective. While Shylock is not swayed by her speech, the audience's sympathies are more likely than ever to lie with Antonio after she has described mercy using a simple **simile** inspired by natural world: 'It droppeth as the gentle rain from heaven/Upon the place beneath' (lines 183–84). She says that mercy is 'mightiest in the mightiest' (line 186) and that it 'blesseth him that gives, and him that takes' (line 185), suggesting that the merciful path is more noble and godly than the pursuit of 'justice' at all costs. Portia uses several words associated with Christianity such as 'heaven' (line 183), 'blest' (line 184), 'salvation' (line 198) and 'prayer' (line 199), and reminds the courtroom that the Lord's Prayer itself calls for forgiveness: 'that same prayer doth teach us all to render/The deeds of mercy' (lines 199–200). Her intervention **foreshadows** not only Shylock's failure to see justice done (as he sees it), but also Antonio's insistence that Shylock 'presently become a Christian' (line 385).

KEY CONTEXT   (A03)

Portia's words about mercy may have been inspired by the following verse from the Bible: 'Let my teaching fall like rain and my words descend like dew, like showers on new grass, like abundant rain on tender plants.' (Deuteronomy 32:2)

KEY QUOTATION: ANTONIO'S WEAKNESS   (A01)

At the point when Shylock has refused all pleas to spare Antonio, Antonio seems to accept his fate. He tells Bassanio, 'I am a tainted wether of the flock/Meetest for death' (IV.1.114–115). referring to how feeble newborn lambs were sometimes killed to prevent further suffering or to preserve essential food for healthy animals. Some have seen Antonio's behaviour as self-sacrificing – as if he is willing to face death for others. Some point to how he was sad at the start of the play, as if he realised there was some inherent weakness or failing in him. What do you think?

CHECKPOINT 8   (A01)

Who says 'How shalt thou hope for mercy, rendering none?' and to whom is the character speaking?

REVISION FOCUS: STAGING OF THE SCENE

Imagine the expressions of the actors, first as Antonio bares his flesh and prepares to die and then as Portia succeeds in setting a trap for Shylock. Research different productions and consider different ways in which this scene could be staged.

ACT IV SCENE 2: THE WIVES TEST THEIR HUSBANDS

SUMMARY

- Portia and Nerissa are still in Venice, dressed in their disguises. Portia asks Nerissa to find Shylock's house and to get him to sign a deed naming Lorenzo and Jessica as his heirs.
- Gratiano brings Bassanio's ring to Portia. Nerissa thinks it would be amusing to try to get Gratiano to part with the ring that she gave him.
- Portia says that the two women will grow old listening to their husbands swearing that they gave the rings away to men but will 'outface them, and outswear them too' (line 17).

WHY IS THIS SCENE IMPORTANT?

A The **financial future** of Lorenzo and Jessica is secured by Shylock's deed.

B The **ring plot** develops – both Nerissa and Portia have tricked their husbands.

KEY FORM: TRAGICOMEDY A02

Once Portia has defeated Shylock, that element of the plot is over. The play moves from potential tragedy to light humour and it is at this point that *The Merchant of Venice* becomes a tragicomedy. In order for the play to regain a lighter tone after the serious moments in the courtroom, Shakespeare introduces a new plot. This is to revolve around the idea of wives testing their husbands' loyalties. Portia has revealed a conventional side to her nature (in Elizabethan terms) by promising to give herself completely to Bassanio. Here we see the stronger side of Portia's nature as she prepares with Nerissa to outwit their new husbands.

TOP TIP A01

Notice how Portia moves very quickly from pursuing Shylock to arranging an elaborate practical joke. The fate of Shylock does not appear to trouble her conscience.

TOP TIP A01

The setting for this short scene is again Venice, but on a street rather than in the courtroom. Make sure you know where each scene happens and how Shakespeare uses the different settings.

ACT V SCENE 1: RESOLUTION

SUMMARY

- Lorenzo and Jessica are interrupted by the arrival of Stephano, bringing news that Portia will arrive home before dawn.
- Lancelot stumbles around in the dark looking for Lorenzo, finds him and announces that Bassanio is also due home before daybreak.
- Portia and Nerissa arrive to find that Bassanio and Gratiano are not yet there. Portia gives orders that no one should mention that the women have also been away.
- The husbands arrive with Antonio.
- Nerissa has challenged Gratiano as to why he is not wearing the ring she gave him, and accuses him of having given it to a woman – which, of course, he has. Portia joins in the joke and says that she gave a ring to Bassanio but he would never have given his away.
- Gratiano swears that Bassanio gave his ring to the judge while he gave his to the clerk. Portia adds to her husband's discomfort by saying that she will never sleep with him until she has seen the ring and Nerissa promises the same to Gratiano.
- Bassanio begs Portia to believe that he has not given the ring to a woman.
- The situation is taken one stage further when Portia insists 'I'll have that doctor for my bedfellow' (line 233) and Nerissa says she will sleep with the clerk. Antonio feels that he must intervene to support his friends, at which point Portia produces Bassanio's ring and says that she was given it by the doctor after having slept with him. The men are amazed at their wives' behaviour.
- Portia finally gives them a letter from Doctor Bellario explaining that she had been the lawyer and Nerissa her clerk.
- Portia also gives Antonio a letter which tells him that three of his ships have arrived safely.

CHECKPOINT 9 **A01**

Who says to whom: 'Were you the clerk that is to make me cuckold'?

WHY IS THIS SCENE IMPORTANT?

A The focus returns to the play's more **tranquil setting of Belmont**, and specifically to Portia's garden there.
B The husbands are forced to admit they **gave their rings away** and Portia and Nerissa **exploit the situation**.
C **Harmony and happiness** are restored – but **not for Shylock**.

TOP TIP: WRITING ABOUT PORTIA (A01)

It is important to consider different interpretations of characters' motives. It is difficult to know how long Portia has had the letter with the good news about Antonio's ships – and where did she get it from? If she already knew the contents of the letter, consider what this says about her. What do you think motivates Portia in the trial scene?

KEY LANGUAGE: COURTLY LOVE (A02)

In this scene, the characters behave in a manner dictated by the idea of courtly love. This literary convention demanded that lovers spoke and acted in certain ways and indeed Lorenzo and Jessica speak in this scene like typical lovers. Note the poetic repetition of the phrase 'In such a night' (lines 1, 6, 9, 12, 14 and so on) and other examples of rather flowery or formal diction, for example 'When the sweet wind did gently kiss the trees' (line 2) and 'But hark, I hear the footing of a man' (line 24). The classical stories to which they allude, however, deal with the pain, tragedy and betrayal of love as well as the ecstasy, and perhaps link to the combination of comedy and tragedy in the play overall.

KEY FORM: COMEDY AND TRAGEDY (A02)

All of the elements of the plot have been neatly tied up. The play is given a light-hearted, happy ending in keeping with Shakespeare's intention for it to be a comedy. However, it is interesting to consider what Shylock – whose final words within the play are spoken in Act IV – might be doing at this point in the play. As with traditional tragic heroes such as Othello and Macbeth, Shakespeare has documented this character's downfall in considerable detail. A recent production at the Globe Theatre starring Jonathan Pryce added an epilogue – a short, wordless scene showing Shylock being baptised while Jessica sings. This is just one way in which the audience might be reminded of Shylock's downfall, and of the actions and attitudes that led to his downfall, at the end of the play.

KEY CONTEXT (A03)

There are several classical allusions to lovers in this final scene, including Troilus and Cressida, Thisbe (and Pyramus), Dido (and Aeneas), and Endymion (and Diana).

KEY CONTEXT (A03)

Elizabethans believed that the movement of the planets created beautiful harmonies, also known as the 'music of the spheres'. The music in this scene reflects the romantic mood at the end of the play and the restoration of order.

PROGRESS AND REVISION CHECK

SECTION ONE: CHECK YOUR KNOWLEDGE

Answer these quick questions to test your basic knowledge of the play, its characters and events:

1. Why does Bassanio need money at the start of the play?

2. Why does Portia have to use the casket test to find a husband?

3. Why does Antonio not have the money available to lend to Bassanio?

4. What word for a legal agreement does Shylock repeatedly use to refer to his insurance against the loan?

5. Who leaves Shylock's service and who does he start to work for instead?

6. To which religion does Jessica convert when she marries Lorenzo?

7. What is inside the gold casket?

8. What kind of party does Bassanio invite his friends to?

9. Who doesn't recognise his own son?

10. Who chooses the silver casket?

11. What is an 'argosy'?

12. What does the silver casket contain?

13. What does Jessica take with her when she elopes?

14. What must the suitors do before they choose a casket?

15. Which casket contains Portia's picture?

16. Who is the most senior figure at the trial in Act IV?

17. What does Portia say Shylock may not do when he takes his 'pound of flesh' (IV.1.230)?

18. What is the 'balance' referred to in the trial scene?

19. With what item do Portia and Nerissa trick their husbands at the end of the play?

20. In which location does the play end?

SECTION TWO: CHECK YOUR UNDERSTANDING

Here are two tasks about the significance of particular moments in the play. These require more thought and slightly longer responses. In each case, try to write at least three to four paragraphs.

Task 1: Look again at the opening of the play, and in particular the conversation between Bassanio and Antonio. What is significant about this conversation? Think about:

- what we learn about some of the play's main characters
- how the events in this scene set other events in motion.

Task 2: Comment on the importance of Portia's judgement at the end of the trial in Act IV Scene 1. Think about:

- parallels and contrasts that could be drawn with other events in the play
- the effects of this judgement on Shylock and Antonio.

PROGRESS CHECK

GOOD PROGRESS

I can:

- understand how Shakespeare has sequenced and revealed events. ☐
- refer to the importance of key events in the play. ☐
- select well-chosen evidence, including key quotations, to support my ideas. ☐

EXCELLENT PROGRESS

I can:

- refer in depth to main and minor events and how they contribute to the development of the plot. ☐
- understand how Shakespeare has carefully ordered or revealed events for particular effects. ☐
- draw on a range of carefully selected key evidence, including quotations, to support my ideas. ☐

WHO'S WHO?

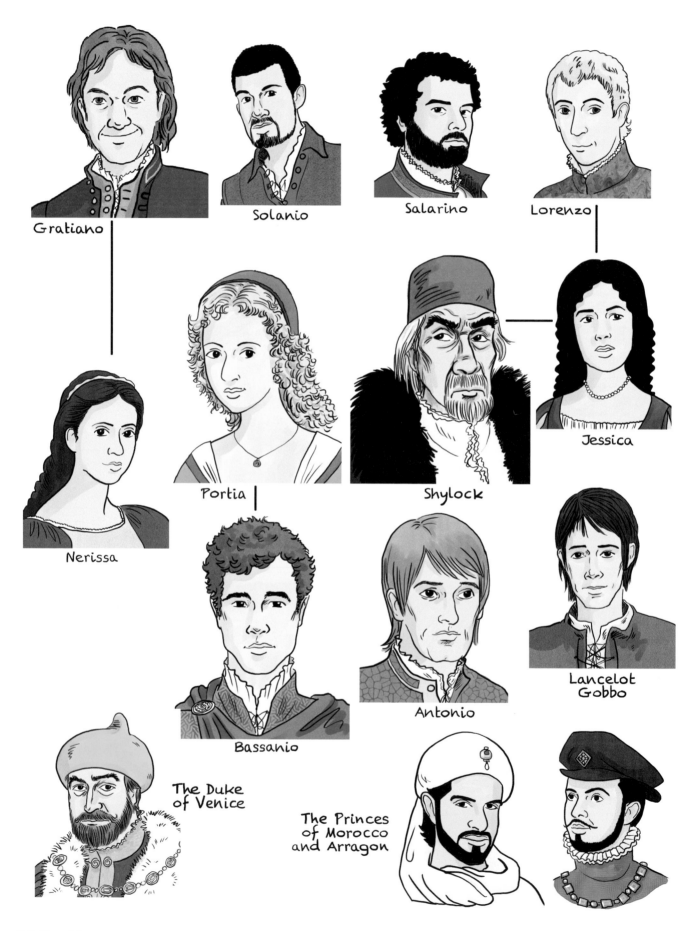

Gratiano

Solanio

Salarino

Lorenzo

Nerissa

Portia

Shylock

Jessica

Bassanio

Antonio

Lancelot Gobbo

The Duke of Venice

The Princes of Morocco and Arragon

ANTONIO

ANTONIO'S ROLE IN THE PLAY

Antonio is the 'merchant of Venice' of the play's title. While he is not actually a member of the aristocracy like the Duke, he is a much-respected member of the merchant class in Venice. During the play:

- He borrows money from Shylock in order to support his friend Bassanio.
- His survival relies on the safe return of his ships.
- He comes close to losing his life but Portia successfully intervenes.

EXAM FOCUS: WRITING ABOUT ANTONIO

Key point	Evidence/further meaning
• Antonio is wealthy, well known and influential.	• The behaviour of Salarino and Solanio in Act I Scene 1 suggests that Antonio's friendship and patronage are well worth having.
• He is loyal to his friends, particularly Bassanio.	• Antonio lends Bassanio money freely and willingly. • He is, quite literally, prepared to die for his friend.
• Perhaps paradoxically, he is also a rather solitary figure.	• He is melancholy at the start of the play: 'such a want-wit sadness makes of me' (I.1.6). • Unlike many of the other characters, Antonio does not find love at the end of the play.
• He respects the law, which ultimately is on his side.	• He seems resigned to his fate at Shylock's hand: 'The duke cannot deny the course of law' (III.3.26). • Once his own life has been spared, he returns to persecuting Shylock.

TOP TIP: ANTONIO'S TREATMENT OF SHYLOCK (A01)

Antonio's treatment of his friend Bassanio is in stark contrast to his treatment of Shylock. Shylock says of Antonio, 'I hate him for he is a Christian' (I.3.38) and plans to take revenge upon him for the ill-treatment that he has received from the Christians. (At the time the play was written, Christians could attack Jews openly, whereas the laws of Venice prohibited Jews from retaliating.) Shylock describes how Antonio has often insulted Shylock in public because of his occupation as a moneylender, called him 'misbeliever' (I.3.106) because of his Jewish faith, spat upon his coat and in his face, and kicked him as though he were a dog. Far from denying these accusations, Antonio angrily says he would do the same again. Even at the point of asking for money, Antonio is immovable in his view of Shylock as an enemy.

KEY CONTEXT (A03)

A wealthy person who takes someone under his wing is known as a patron, and Antonio behaves as Bassanio's patron.

PORTIA

PORTIA'S ROLE IN THE PLAY

Portia is a wealthy heiress living outside Venice in Belmont with Nerissa and her other servants. During the play:

- She is bound by the terms of her father's will as to her choice of husband.
- She is relieved when Morocco and Arragon fail to win her hand in marriage, and is delighted by Bassanio's success in selecting the right casket.
- She disguises herself as the lawyer Balthazar and cleverly wins Antonio his freedom.
- She and Nerissa play tricks on their new husbands after the trial to test their loyalty.

PORTIA'S IMPORTANCE TO THE PLAY AS A WHOLE

Portia is a strong character. Shakespeare often portrays women as being more clever and resourceful than men, and this play is no exception. Many of the play's scenes are set in Belmont and tell the story of Portia and her suitors. In the second half of the play, the worlds of Belmont and Venice become more closely interwoven as Bassanio wins Portia's hand in marriage, and Portia goes to the aid of her new husband's friend. Portia provides the play with much of its comedy, as well as being involved in its more serious themes.

AIMING HIGH: PORTIA IN LOVE

The very best answers will look at different aspects of a character and how they develop throughout the play. Once Bassanio has chosen the correct casket, Portia's language and attitude are more modest and coy than in previous scenes, and she immediately tells Bassanio that she is his to command as he is now her 'king' (III.2.165). This is in contrast to the sharp-tongued woman who gave such a harsh description of her suitors! We might have expected Portia to keep Bassanio waiting, but she marries him at once. It seems that to a certain extent she is a conventional Elizabethan woman. However, her treatment of Bassanio after the trial is further evidence of her mischievous wit. She knows that it will be difficult for Bassanio to give up the ring she has given him yet, in her disguise as Balthazar, she insists upon it.

In Act V, Portia takes great delight in making her husband feel uncomfortable and a parallel could be drawn with Shylock's treatment of Antonio, in that she tricks Bassanio into swearing to a bond that she doubts he'll be able to keep and then torments him for breaking it. Portia seems very much in control of the marriage, despite her earlier statement that Bassanio is her lord.

KEY CONTEXT (A03)

When Portia says Morocco has 'the complexion of a devil' (I.2.119) and 'Let all of his complexion choose me so' (II.7.79), her words reflect the attitudes that were prevalent in Shakespeare's time.

EXAM FOCUS: WRITING ABOUT PORTIA

Key point	Evidence/further meaning
● Portia is loyal to her dead father and his wishes.	● She promises: 'I will die as chaste as Diana unless I be obtained by the manner of my father's will' (I.2.98–100).
● She is intelligent and resourceful.	● She devises a plan to help Antonio and acts decisively to set her plan in motion: 'I have work in hand/That you yet know not of' (III.4.57–8).
● She is mischievous and witty.	● She mocks her suitors as she describes them to her friend and confidante Nerissa, asking her to assess her 'affection' for each man 'according to my description' (I.2.35–6)
● She is worldly and can make crude remarks.	● She plays suggestively on the idea of Nerissa and herself appearing 'accomplished/With that we lack' (III.5.61–2) when dressed as men (i.e. without male genitalia).

TOP TIP (A01)

Be prepared to examine Portia's complex character in some depth. She has been praised as Shakespeare's first great female character.

TOP TIP: WRITING ABOUT PORTIA (A02)

Make sure you can write about Portia's wit (her intellect). It is her finest quality. She can argue better than any other character in the play, and it is difficult to imagine anyone outdoing her. This is shown most clearly in the trial scene. Portia outwits Shylock by encouraging him to insist that his bond is followed to the letter.

Her appeal for mercy is moving, accomplished and extremely effective. This speech encourages the audience to be on the side of the Christians and to view Shylock as a wicked man. Although she teaches the courtroom about mercy earlier in the scene, Portia insists upon Shylock's goods and lands being seized. She wants him to beg the Duke for his life and seems to delight in humiliating him. Examine Portia's language closely in Act IV Scene 1, analysing the techniques she uses to argue and persuade with authority.

SHYLOCK

SHYLOCK'S ROLE IN THE PLAY

Shylock is a Jewish moneylender. During the play:

- He lends Antonio the money that Bassanio needs.
- The bond they agree places Antonio's life at risk.
- He is devastated when his daughter leaves his household.
- He describes how he has been persecuted by Christians.
- He relishes the chance to take his 'pound of flesh' (IV.1.230) by legal means – but ultimately the law thwarts him, and it is he who is punished in the final settlement.

SHYLOCK'S IMPORTANCE TO THE PLAY AS A WHOLE

CHECKPOINT 10 (A01)

Who calls Shylock an 'inhuman wretch'?

Shylock's character can be interpreted in different ways. He is the villain whose comeuppance means that the play can reach its satisfying conclusion. However, Shakespeare's characterisation means that modern audiences usually feel sympathy for him and see his lust for revenge as a reaction to his harsh and unfair treatment.

EXAM FOCUS: WRITING ABOUT SHYLOCK (A01)

Key point	Evidence/further meaning
● Shylock is true to his faith.	● Shylock says in Act I 'I will not eat with you, drink with you, nor pray with you' (I.3.32–3) and accuses Antonio of hating 'our sacred nation' (I.3.43).
● He has been a victim of prejudice and mistreatment for a long time.	● Shylock complains about how Antonio has treated him in public 'many a time and oft' (I.3.101).
● He is unpopular in his own household.	● Jessica escapes Shylock's household. ● Lancelot Gobbo complains that he is 'famished in his service' (II.2.99).
● He can seem driven by hatred and rage to the point of obsession.	● In Act III Scene 3 he interrupts Antonio and repeatedly insists 'I'll have my bond; I will not hear thee speak' (III.3.12). ● When Portia suggests that he should be merciful, he replies 'On what compulsion must I? Tell me that' (IV.1.181).
● He can be very eloquent about his situation.	● In his 'I am a Jew. Hath not a Jew eyes?' speech (III.1.52–65), he speaks movingly about what all men have in common, irrespective of race or religion.

KEY CONTEXT: PERFORMING SHYLOCK (A03)

The way in which Shylock is portrayed on stage has changed considerably since the play was first performed, when he appeared as a villain and a clown. This change took place in the nineteenth century when the actor Edmund Kean played Shylock as an intelligent man who had been victimised. Certainly Shakespeare did not write Shylock as a simple, one-dimensional part. He is one of the most complex characters in English literature. To a modern audience, Shylock is sometimes a victim and sometimes a villain. Elizabethans would have held the much simpler view that the Christians were right and so Shylock was in the wrong.

AIMING HIGH: A SYMPATHETIC CHARACTER? ★

For very high marks you need to develop a personal interpretation of a key character like Shylock, and justify your view with evidence from the play. For example, you could argue that Shylock is not to blame for his behaviour. We first see him when Bassanio and Antonio ask him for the loan of 3,000 ducats. Shylock is clearly plotting his revenge on Antonio, but we soon sympathise with him because of Antonio's bullying.

Other characters add to this view that Shylock is victimised. Salarino and Solanio behave like Antonio, Launcelot leaves his service and even his own daughter deserts him. Apart from two brief episodes with Tubal, we never see Shylock with his own people, so we are usually given the Christians view of him. The Christians' invite him to dinner on the night that Jessica elopes with Lorenzo, and so betray his trust further.

Shylock does, however, pursue his revenge upon Antonio. The lines 'I'll plague him, I'll torture him. I am glad of it' (III.1.103–4) show how bitter Shylock has become, yet we cannot help but feel that this is not all his fault. After years of being kicked and spat upon by men like Antonio, Shylock's hatred is understandable. Do you agree? What other arguments could you make?

Engraving showing Lopez (right) plotting with a Spanish emissary to poison Elizabeth I

TOP TIP (A01)

It might seem odd that Shylock does not appear in the final act of the play. Look closely at his final remarks and consider the final impression an audience might have of him on stage. What do you think this suggests about his position in society?

KEY CONTEXT (A03)

Although Jews had been expelled from England in 1290, there were exceptions who claimed to be Christians to avoid persecution. Queen Elizabeth had some Jewish ladies-in-waiting and a Jewish physician named Roderigo Lopez who entered her service in 1581. Dr Lopez was eventually charged with plotting to poison her, and was executed in 1594. Some researchers have speculated as to whether Lopez was an inspiration for the character of Shylock.

BASSANIO

BASSANIO'S ROLE IN THE PLAY

Bassanio is a Venetian gentleman and close friend of Antonio's. During the play:

- He asks Antonio for money to help him win Portia's hand in marriage.
- He goes to Belmont and is successful in the casket test.
- He tries to help Antonio in his hour of need.

CHECKPOINT 11 (A01)

What 'steals the colour from Bassanio's cheek' in Act III Scene 2?

BASSANIO'S IMPORTANCE TO THE PLAY AS A WHOLE

Bassanio's story is central to the whole play. The loan that Antonio takes out on his behalf puts Antonio's life in danger. However Portia – the reason Bassanio sought the money in the first place – comes to Antonio's aid in the trial scene.

EXAM FOCUS: WRITING ABOUT BASSANIO

Key point	Evidence/further meaning
● Bassanio is a true and loyal friend to Antonio.	● He is wary of Shylock and doesn't want Antonio to enter into an agreement with the Jew that puts his life at risk. ● He leaves his wife on their wedding day to travel to Venice and help Antonio. ● In the trial scene, he offers to exchange his life for Antonio's.
● He has a reputation for spending money and amassing debt.	● At the start of the play he says that he has wasted all his own fortune and a sum of money loaned to him by Antonio.
● He shows good judgement in choosing the lead casket.	● He speaks wisely about appearance and reality: 'There is no vice so simple but assumes/Some mark of virtue on his outward parts' (III.2.81–2).
● However, he can also be rather naïve.	● His optimistic nature is evident from the very first scene, when he describes why he should be allowed to borrow money even though he has already lost so much. ● He thinks that he can simply talk Shylock out of taking the 'pound of flesh' (IV.1.230). He does not seem to realise the strength of the moneylender's feelings and so misjudges the situation.

AIMING HIGH: PLOT AND CHARACTER

For the very best grades you'll need to show you have an overview of the play as a whole, and how Shakespeare constructs the story. For example, notice how Shakespeare helps the audience to make the connection between the play's different plots by mentioning Bassanio in Act I Scene 2. There is an instant contrast between the mocking, dismissive way in which the other suitors are described and Portia's evident interest in Bassanio, despite her attempts to conceal her interest: 'Yes, yes, it was Bassanio! – as I think so was he called' (I.2.106). Bassanio is portrayed in this brief description as a perfect suitor – 'a scholar and a soldier' (I.2.104) with noble and worthy friends and, it is hinted, a handsome man: 'of all the men that ever my foolish eyes looked upon was the best deserving a fair lady' (I.2.107–108). The suggestion is that this man is likely to be a successful suitor, but of course it is only as a result of Antonio's money – requested in Scene 1 and secured in Scene 3 – that Bassanio is able to come to Belmont to attempt the casket test.

TOP TIP: COMPARING BASSANIO AND PORTIA (A01)

It can be useful to compare Bassanio and Portia. Although Bassanio has the upper hand in marriage due to his gender (being the man), Shakespeare shows him to be more straightforward and less capable than his wife. He is troubled when he has to give his ring to the lawyer and yet he does so because he feels it is the right thing to do. When Portia presses him for an explanation as to why he is not wearing the ring, he tells the truth. He could have made up a story or have simply said that he had lost it; instead he confesses to having given it away to the first person who asked for it. Compare this with Portia's strategic mind and elaborate plotting in the second half of the play.

TOP TIP (A01)

During the trial, Bassanio has difficulty keeping his temper, calling Shylock a 'cruel devil' (IV.1.215). However, he still hopes that Shylock can be won round by argument and persuasion. How would you describe Bassanio in this scene?

GRATIANO

GRATIANO'S ROLE IN THE PLAY

Gratiano is a Venetian gentleman. During the play:

- He spends time with his friends Bassanio, Lorenzo, Solanio and Salarino.
- He falls in love with Nerissa.
- He verbally attacks Shylock.

EXAM FOCUS: WRITING ABOUT GRATIANO

Key point	Evidence/further meaning
• Gratiano is viewed as a clown and is known to be talkative.	• After a long speech by Gratiano in Act I Scene 1, Lorenzo says 'Gratiano never lets me speak' (I.1.107) and Bassanio says that 'Gratiano speaks an infinite deal of nothing' (I.1.114).
• He is impulsive.	• He falls in love with Nerissa in the time it takes Bassanio to choose the casket: 'You saw the mistress, I beheld the maid' (III.2.198). • He also promises never to remove the ring he has been given without thinking through the consequences.
• He insults Shylock.	• He calls Shylock an 'inexecrable dog' (IV.1.128).

TOP TIP: GRATIANO THE JOKER (A01)

You could think of Gratiano as the class joker. He is looked upon by his friends as a clown. He talks far too much and not always at the appropriate time. Bassanio has been in trouble in the past because of Gratiano's behaviour and is sometimes embarrassed by him. Gratiano cannot resist the temptation to make a joke whenever possible and loves the sound of his own voice.

KEY QUOTATION: THE LAST WORD (A01)

It is Gratiano who has the last word in the play: 'Well, while I live I'll fear no other thing/So sore as keeping safe Nerissa's ring.' (V.1.306–7) Notice that this is a **rhyming couplet**, a technique commonly used to emphasise that a scene is being brought to a close.

JESSICA

JESSICA'S ROLE IN THE PLAY

Jessica is Shylock's daughter. During the play:

- She complains about her father.
- She escapes by eloping with Lorenzo.
- She marries and converts to Christianity.

EXAM FOCUS: WRITING ABOUT JESSICA

Key point	Evidence/further meaning
● Jessica disowns her father to be with the man she loves.	● The audience witnesses her elopement in Act II. She disguises herself as a page boy to make her escape. ● Jessica speaks of her intention to marry Lorenzo: 'If thou keep promise, I shall end this strife,/Become a Christian and thy loving wife.' (II.3.19–20)
● She takes some of Shylock's wealth with her.	● Her treatment of Shylock can be seen as cruel; not only does she steal from Shylock, she spends his money freely in Genoa.
● She may still be seen as an outsider by her Christian friends.	● Even though Jessica converts to Christianity, she is largely ignored by the other characters – especially Portia – in the scenes at Belmont. This could suggest they haven't fully accepted her.

TOP TIP A01

Consider how sympathetically Shakespeare presents both Jessica's plight, and her revenge on her father.

LORENZO

LORENZO'S ROLE IN THE PLAY

Lorenzo is another Venetian gentleman. During the play:

- He is friends with Bassanio, Gratiano, Solanio and Salarino.
- He falls in love with Jessica and they elope together.
- The couple end the play in Belmont with Portia.

EXAM FOCUS: WRITING ABOUT LORENZO

Key point	Evidence/further meaning
• Lorenzo falls in love with Jessica.	• He calls Jessica 'gentle' (II.4.19) and 'Fair' (II.4.39).
• He marries Jessica who converts to Christianity.	• He describes Jessica as 'issue to a faithless Jew' (II.4.37).
• He and Jessica will inherit Shylock's wealth when he dies.	• Antonio says that Shylock should 'record a gift,/Here in this court, of all he lies possess'd/Unto his son Lorenzo and his daughter' (IV.1.386–8).

AIMING HIGH: HAPPY ENDINGS?

Consider what Shakespeare tells us about Lorenzo and Jessica's relationship. A Christian and Bassanio's associate, Lorenzo has fallen in love with Jessica, though it is unlikely that they could have met frequently as they come from different cultures. He takes her away from Venice without having made specific plans. They roam Italy spending huge sums of money unwisely and then arrive in Belmont and stay in the house of someone neither of them know. This suggests that Lorenzo has not planned their future and has failed to consider how a Christian with a Jewish wife will be received. Perhaps the conversation about doomed classical lovers such as Dido who 'Stood … with a willow in her hand/Upon the wild sea banks, and waft her love/To come again to Carthage' (V.1.10–12) is more relevant than he thinks.

NERISSA

NERISSA'S ROLE IN THE PLAY

Nerissa lives in Belmont with Portia. She is Portia's lady-in-waiting. During the play:

- She attends to Portia and keeps her company.
- She dresses as a lawyer's clerk as part of Portia's plan to save Antonio from Shylock's bond.
- She marries Gratiano and plays a trick on him.

EXAM FOCUS: WRITING ABOUT NERISSA

Key point	Evidence/further meaning
• Nerissa is close to Portia.	• The two women speak in prose in Act I Scene 2 and their language shows their familiarity and the ease with which they speak to one another.
• She sometimes asserts herself with her mistress.	• When Portia is complaining about her situation in Act I Scene 2, Nerissa counsels her mistress to follow her advice.
• Like Portia, she plays a trick on her husband.	• She reminds Gratiano that he swore that he would wear her ring 'till your hour of death,/And that it should lie with you in your grave.' (V.1.153–4)

REVISION FOCUS: NERISSA AND PORTIA

Make a list of all the times that Portia and Nerissa speak to each other, and what this tells you about their relationship. You might find that:

- Nerissa generally follows what her mistress asks and does, and her intense loyalty to her mistress is never in question.
- However, she does show her independence by being prepared to put Portia in her place when she starts to complain about her life.
- By the end of the play she, like Portia, is married and the test of the rings can be seen as a commentary on the question of loyalty in marriage, a key theme of the play.

In this way Shakespeare continues to make connections between the two women and to demonstrate their closeness and their enduring friendship as married women.

TOP TIP **A01**

Nerissa is present in some scenes in which she has little or nothing to say. How might she be acting and reacting to events on stage?

KEY CONTEXT (A03)

The stage direction for Act II Scene 2 describes Gobbo as *'the Clown'*, strongly suggesting that the part may have originally been written by Shakespeare with the popular comic actor Will Kemp in mind.

TOP TIP (A01)

Make a list of the characters who are present in each scene as you read and revise it. Take note of the minor characters, including Shylock's friend Tubal, the jailer, servants, messengers, court officials and musicians. What is their role?

MINOR CHARACTERS

LANCELOT AND OLD GOBBO

Lancelot is a comic character who represents the ordinary citizens of Venice. He is only interested in the lives and livelihoods of Bassanio and the others when they directly affect him. He happily moves from one master (Shylock) to another (Bassanio) to improve his situation. He criticises Shylock, but is devoted to Jessica and has formed a genuine friendship with her. He serves to lighten the atmosphere of the play and his appearances tend to follow particularly dramatic moments. He also gives the other characters, such as Lorenzo, someone to make fun of.

Old Gobbo, Lancelot's father, is nearly blind and easily confused. He fails at first to recognise his own son, but tries to help Lancelot to obtain a position with Bassanio. He often chooses the wrong word for the occasion, with comic effect.

SALARINO AND SOLANIO

These two men are quite wealthy citizens, though they are clearly looking for an opportunity to better themselves. They see Antonio as a useful person to know and are rather jealous of the attention that he shows to Bassanio. They frequently act as reporters of off-stage action, filling in information on events that would have taken too long to portray on stage. They also reinforce the strongly anti-Semitic atmosphere of Venice in their unpleasant comments about Shylock.

THE PRINCES OF MOROCCO AND ARRAGON

A proud man who feels that he has as much right to marry Portia as anyone, Morocco is pompous and full of himself but proves to be honourable. In Act II Scene 1, he describes his appearance and his conduct in heroic terms, with references to a 'lion' (II.1.30) and to the classical hero 'Hercules' (II.1.32). Depending on how the part is performed, this could present Morocco as a fool or as an important man who suffers discrimination at the hands of Portia.

Arragon speaks in a long-winded way and is full of his own importance. It should be remembered that Ar(r)agon was a Spanish kingdom and that the English and the Spanish had been bitter enemies for many years at the time the play was written. The Prince of Arragon is an Englishman's stereotypical idea of a Spaniard. In Act II Scene 9, he sees himself as better than 'the barbarous multitudes' (II.9.32) but, like Morocco, his proud boasting comes before a fall.

THE DUKE

As ruler of the city-state of Venice, the Duke is the most powerful and wealthy man in the city and has the final say in major disputes. He appears to be fair, as he does not want to see Antonio killed, but equally, he will not break the laws of Venice simply to defeat Shylock. It could be argued that this makes him a poor ruler as he is not prepared to sacrifice his own reputation in order to see that justice prevails.

PROGRESS AND REVISION CHECK

SECTION ONE: CHECK YOUR KNOWLEDGE

Answer these quick questions to test your basic knowledge of the play's characters:

1. Who does Lancelot Gobbo leave Shylock's service to go to work for?
2. What is the name of Shylock's Jewish friend?
3. Which suitor takes the casket test first?
4. To whom does Portia ask Balthazar to take a letter?
5. Who reports that Shylock was heard to moan 'O my ducats! O my daughter!'?
6. Who does Lorenzo marry?
7. 'He was wont to call me usurer.' Who is Shylock talking about?
8. Who give away their rings much to their wives' displeasure?
9. Who says 'Thou shalt have justice more than thou desirest'?
10. Margery and Leah don't appear in the play but are mentioned. Who are they?

SECTION TWO: CHECK YOUR UNDERSTANDING.

Task: To what extent would you describe Shakespeare's portrayal of Shylock as sympathetic?

Consider:

- how Shylock speaks about his own situation
- how other characters speak about and treat him.

TOP TIP (A01)

This task requires more thought and a slightly longer response. Try to write at least three to four paragraphs.

PROGRESS CHECK

GOOD PROGRESS

I can:

- explain the significance of the main characters in how the action develops ☐
- refer to how they are described by Shakespeare and how this affects the way we see them. ☐

EXCELLENT PROGRESS

I can:

- analyse in detail how Shakespeare has shaped and developed characters over the course of the play ☐
- infer key ideas, themes and issues from the ways characters and relationships are presented by Shakespeare. ☐

THEME TRACKER (A01)

Money and commerce

- Act I Scene 1 line 138–9: Antonio says his 'purse …/ Lie[s] all unlock'd' for Bassanio to use.
- Act I Scene 3: Antonio, Bassanio and Shylock negotiate the terms of the loan.
- Act III Scene 2 line 101: Bassanio rejects 'gaudy gold' in favour of the less valuable lead casket.

CHECKPOINT 12 (A01)

What is Shylock's complaint when he says Antonio 'lends out money gratis' (I.3.39)?

THEME TRACKER (A01)

Love and marriage

- Act II Scene 9: Portia and Nerissa eagerly anticipate Bassanio's arrival.
- Act II Scenes 5 and 6: Jessica elopes with Lorenzo.
- Act III Scene 2 lines 166–7: Portia tells her Bassanio that 'Myself, and what is mine, to you and yours/Is now converted.'

THEMES

MONEY AND COMMERCE

Throughout the play, money is woven into characters' lives and relationships in complex ways:

- In the play's first scene, Antonio describes his sadness using imagery that has connotations of something material and measurable like money: 'how I caught it, found it, or came by it,/What stuff 'tis made of, whereof it is born' (I.1.3–4).
- The play is set in the world of trade and commerce, with powerful merchants' fortunes dependent on powers beyond their control. Salarino's description of 'dangerous rocks', of spices 'on the stream' and waters robed with 'my silks' sets a tone of impending disaster, indicating that fortunes can be lost as well as won: 'even now worth this,/And now worth nothing' (I.1.31–7).

- The marriage plot involving Portia is about financial transactions and how wealth moves between generations, as much as it is about love.
- The situations of all the key characters are precarious but none more so than Shylock whose wealth cannot insure him against intolerance and hatred.

LOVE AND MARRIAGE

The love and marriage plot is woven around the main plot of the bond agreed between Antonio and Shylock:

- During the play, three couples marry: Portia and Bassanio, Nerissa and Gratiano, and Jessica and Lorenzo.
- The plot involving Portia, her suitors and the caskets unfolds over five acts and is the source of much humour in the play.
- Over the course of the play, the suitors become newlyweds, and the vows of marriage which they have exchanged are examined and put to another kind of test when two of the husbands break their vows by giving away their rings.
- While this particular predicament is soon solved, there are other unresolved questions, for example, why Portia's father wished to dictate her choice of husband from beyond the grave, the extent to which Lorenzo and Jessica will ever become fully accepted by Christian society, and what Antonio will do now that his best friend is married.

PREJUDICE AND DISCRIMINATION

This theme is centred around the Jewish characters and how they relate to the Christian characters, but also relates to other 'outsiders' such as the Princes of Morocco and Arragon. It is also connected to the theme of appearance and reality in terms of how far characters are judged on the basis of their physical appearance and their beliefs, and according to others' prejudiced views of them:

- The inscription in Morocco's choice of casket reads 'All that glisters is not gold' (II.7.65). For a play that offers wisdom about looking beyond appearances, there are many cases of characters failing to follow this advice.

- Portia makes up her mind about her suitors after having met them only briefly. In the case of Morocco, she gives an opinion of him before she has even seen him, and meeting him serves to strengthen her prejudice: 'Let all of his complexion choose me so' (II.7.79).

- The two failed suitors, Morocco and Arragon, go on to make the mistake of choosing a casket based on outward appearances, while Bassanio is seen to possess the wisdom to choose 'meagre lead' (III.2.104).

- To a modern audience, Portia's use of crude cultural stereotypes in describing her suitors, and the insults hurled at Shylock throughout the play, are deeply troubling.

- An audience of the 1590s might have found humour and enjoyment in defeating a villain; today we are more likely to experience **pathos** and feel pity for Shylock, remembering Shylock's tragedy in the midst of the play's comic resolution.

THEME TRACKER (A01)

Prejudice and discrimination

- Act I Scene 2: Portia mocks her suitors.
- Act I Scene 3: Shylock describes how Antonio has treated him.
- Act II Scene 8 lines 4 and 14: Solanio calls Shylock 'The villain Jew' and 'the dog Jew'.

KEY CONTEXT (A03)

The Royal Shakespeare Company's 1987 production with Antony Sher as Shylock featured swastikas and anti-Semitic propaganda scrawled on the walls of Venice.

KEY QUOTATION: PORTIA'S USE OF DISGUISE (A01)

In Act III Scene 4, Portia describes to Nerissa her plan that they should both dress as young men. She says to Nerissa 'When we are both accoutred like young men/I'll prove the prettier fellow of the two,/And wear my dagger with the braver grace' (III.4.63–5). The language Portia uses here suggests she relishes not only disguising herself as a man, but also speaking and behaving as a man. Her disguise will give her new freedom and the licence to act more confidently and extrovertly than was possible for women in Shakespeare's time. She plans to adopt a 'manly stride' and to behave like a 'bragging youth' who tells 'quaint lies' (III.4.68–9). Shakespeare uses the concept of disguise to explore the differences between the sexes here, in a way that is both amusing and thought-provoking.

THEME TRACKER (A01)

Revenge and forgiveness

- Act III Scene 1 line 84: Shylock is angry that that there will be 'no satisfaction, no revenge' after his daughter disappears with many of his riches.
- Act III Scene 3: Shylock repeatedly states that he will redeem his bond.
- Act IV Scene 1 lines 182–203: Portia describes 'the quality of mercy'.

REVENGE AND FORGIVENESS

This theme occurs in different forms in the play:

- From the opening scene onwards, when Antonio helps his friend Bassanio out of trouble once again, the theme of forgiveness is firmly established.
- Shylock is desperate for revenge on Antonio because of the ill treatment that he has suffered. Ultimately, his attempts are frustrated.
- In Act IV Scene 1, the Duke grants Shylock a pardon, but the terms of this pardon – 'you take my life/When you do take the means whereby I live' (IV.1.374–5) – may be seen as more punitive than merciful.
- The matter of the rings in the closing scenes can be seen as a comic exploration of the serious themes of revenge and forgiveness, with Bassanio pleading with his wife that she 'Pardon this fault' and promising that he 'nevermore will break an oath with thee' (V.1.247–8), and all being forgiven at the end of the play.

AIMING HIGH: DOUBLE STANDARDS

Reading beneath the surface is a key skill for higher grades. It could be argued that hypocritical attitudes are in evidence in this play when it comes to revenge and forgiveness. Portia's speech about the 'quality of mercy' (IV.1.182) promotes forgiveness as a Christian virtue, but Antonio's treatment of Shylock in the past has been unkind, and Shylock is not treated mercifully at the end of the play. Does Shakespeare suggest that it is more a matter of who has offended and been offended, than the nature of the offence itself?

CHECKPOINT 13 (A01)

Who calls whom 'worthy judge', 'noble judge' and 'wise and upright judge' in Act IV Scene 1?

KEY QUOTATION: SHYLOCK'S LONG MEMORY (A01)

When the jailer allows Antonio to speak to Shylock, Shylock reminds him: 'Thou call'dst me a dog before thou hadst a cause;/But since I am a dog, beware my fangs' (III.3.6–7). This suggests that Antonio's hatred of Shylock extends back before he had any logical reason (such as the loan) to hate him, thus strengthening the depth of the enmity between them. It suggests tribal hatred which may have its roots in religion or race – or both.

FAMILY

Shakespeare shows us that the bonds between family members can come under immense strain. The complicated relationship between loyalty, love and wealth are explored in many different ways.

- Jessica decides that she is more strongly tied to Lorenzo than to her own father, and appears happy to leave her father's religion too and become a Christian.
- Similarly, Lancelot and his father Gobbo are not close. Gobbo's inability to recognise his own son, while comic, may be viewed as a comment on the tensions and misunderstandings between generations. It may also carry echoes of the parable of the prodigal son.
- Portia's father's will shows his concern to find her a husband who will not marry her just for money. Portia obeys her father's wishes but the process is both amusing and difficult.
- Jessica leaves her father's home with some of his riches, and the settlement following the trial ensures that she and Lorenzo will inherit everything from Shylock when he dies.

REVISION FOCUS: THEME MIND MAP

Try producing a single revision sheet for each theme. Set it out in the form of a mind map with essential quotations and comments of your own.

JUSTICE AND THE LAW

Shakespeare explores the themes of justice and the law throughout the play and raises questions about whether the law in Venice is capable of providing justice:

- Portia's famous speech in Act IV Scene 1 asks for mercy, yet she does not show Shylock any such mercy when she insists on his punishment.
- The outcome of the trial shows that a state's system of justice may uphold the rights of some of its citizens above those of others.
- As ruler, the Duke – who adjudicates at the trial –represents Venetian justice in action.
- Women were excluded from practising the law at this time, leading Portia and Nerissa to dress as male lawyers.

THEME TRACKER (A01)

Friendship

- Act I Scene 3 line 134: Shylock tells Antonio 'I would be friends with you, and have your love'.
- Act II Scene 4: Lorenzo and his friends have dressed up for the masque.
- Act IV Scene 1 lines 280–5: Bassanio speaks of the esteem in which he holds his friend Antonio, and of his wish to 'deliver' him from harm.

FRIENDSHIP

Friendship is one of many bonds between characters that Shakespeare explores in *The Merchant of Venice*. Friendships are shown to inspire virtuous behaviour but they are also put under strain.

- Bassanio is connected to Antonio as a friend and as a debtor, but Antonio says that the friendship between them cancels out the debt.
- Antonio's attitude to his young friend is very generous and self-sacrificing (altruistic) – yet he can treat others badly.
- Bassanio feels responsible when Antonio suffers as a consequence of the bond – and is committed to helping Antonio in his hour of need.
- Later, because of the debt of gratitude that Bassanio owes the lawyer for rescuing his friend, he has to break the promise of loyalty to his wife – not knowing that they are one and the same person.

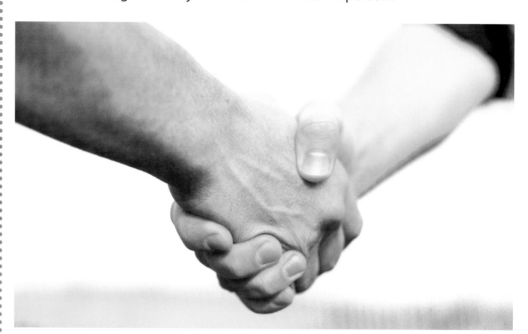

KEY QUOTATION: A PROFOUND FRIENDSHIP (A01)

The extent of Antonio's friendship for Bassanio is astonishing, both in lending him a huge amount of money on a risky business and being prepared to die to pay the debt. Is the 'love' between them reciprocated? Bassanio says in Act 5 Scene 1: '… life itself, my wife, and all the world,/Are not with me esteem'd above thy life' (IV.1.282–283). Would Bassanio have died for Antonio? We will never know.

TOP TIP: LINKS BETWEEN THEMES (A01)

You can also make links *between* themes. Think about the different kinds of bonds that exist between characters in the play: between family members, friends and enemies. What role does money play in these relationships?

CONTEXTS

SHAKESPEARE'S LIFE AND WORKS

Shakespeare was a successful and famous man during his lifetime. He was a favourite playwright of Queen Elizabeth and of her successor, James I. His efforts to please royalty and his links with the Earl of Southampton gave him a privileged position. Shakespeare's plays were well liked by the public and he became very wealthy. It is difficult to think of a modern equivalent of Shakespeare, but world-famous film-makers like Steven Spielberg, Peter Jackson and Tim Burton, or phenomenally successful writers like J. K. Rowling are probably our closest equivalents. By today's standards, Shakespeare was a self-made millionaire, a difficult achievement in the twenty-first century and a remarkable one for the sixteenth. At the time the play was written and first performed in the late 1590s, Elizabeth I was on the throne. Other works from this period in Shakespeare's career include the tragedy *Romeo and Juliet* and the history play *Richard II*.

JEWS IN ENGLAND

The explanation of Shakespeare's portrayal of Shylock is not a simple one. Today we think of different religions living side by side as normal and desirable. This was not the case in Shakespeare's day. For one thing there were virtually no Jews living in England at this time as they had all been taxed to the point of poverty and finally banished, three hundred years before Shakespeare. Shylock is not based upon observations of real Jews. By the time the play was written, only the old, medieval idea of a Jew existed for people in England. The word 'Jew' had come to be applied to hard-hearted, unscrupulous moneylenders, rather than a description of someone's culture and religion.

THE STATUS OF WOMEN

For all Portia's cleverness and independence of spirit, Shakespeare shows us that she is also a dutiful daughter and a devoted wife. For centuries, many upper-class people had their marriages arranged by their parents. A wealthy woman's hand in marriage was accompanied by a large sum of money known as a dowry. This means that the way Portia's father dictates the terms of her marriage from beyond the grave would not have surprised the audience in Shakespeare's time. Instead, it is the theatricality of the casket test that would have caused a stir!

KEY CONTEXT (A03)

The Merchant of Venice was written and first performed in England in the last decade of the sixteenth century. It remains a very well-known and much-debated Shakespeare play today, and Shylock one of Shakespeare's most enduring and troubling dramatic creations.

THE PLAY'S SOURCES

Most of the plot elements of *The Merchant of Venice* appear in stories translated from French and Italian. As there are many similarities between Shakespeare's story and some of these accounts, it seems highly likely that Shakespeare had read, or at least heard of them.

A story in a 1558 collection by Ser Giovanni called *Il Pecorone* (which literally translated means 'the dunce' or 'the blockhead') tells of a wealthy young man named Giannetto visiting the port of Belmont, in a ship supplied by his godfather Ansaldo. There he meets a beautiful, rich widow. He hears that any man who can 'possess' her shall win her wealth and her hand and, to finance his attempt to woo her, he is obliged to borrow money from Ansaldo. As Ansaldo's money is all invested in ventures abroad, he is forced, in turn, to borrow money from a Jewish moneylender. The story of the 'pound of flesh' (IV.1.230) appears here exactly as it does in *The Merchant of Venice*. The story also includes an account of the lady dressing as a lawyer and outwitting the Jewish moneylender, and the business with the rings that occurs in Act V of the play.

KEY CONTEXT (A03)

Italian comedies in the sixteenth century (Commedia dell'Arte) were full of stock characters and plots including witty servants and wealthy older men who object to young lovers marrying. You might trace how Shakespeare has drawn on or developed some of these archetypes.

A likely source for the casket test is an account in *Gesta Romanorum* (translated into English in 1595). Another important influence on Shakespeare's play – and particularly on the characterisation of Shylock – is Christopher Marlowe's 1589 play *The Jew of Malta*.

SETTINGS

VENICE, TRADE AND THE SEA

In Shakespeare's time, Venice, with its famous canals, lagoon and Rialto Bridge, was the most important trading centre in the world. Goods from the Far East were traded in Venice and with them came new ideas and discoveries. The great explorer Marco Polo (1254–1324) was Venetian and he opened up new trade routes with many countries. England was also a major seafaring nation at the time when the play was written, and there are many references to the sea and ships that English audiences would have easily understood. The riches and risks associated with trade-ships are central to the plot of *The Merchant of Venice*; had Antonio's merchant ships travelled safely, Shylock would not have been able to demand revenge. The news that Antonio's ships 'Are richly come to harbour suddenly' (V.1.277) reinforces the idea that his fortunes have improved and adds to the atmosphere of relief and celebration at the end of the play.

THE JEWISH GHETTO

By a decree of 1516, a Venetian city council removed Jewish people from the main part of the city. From the sixteenth to the nineteenth centuries, Jewish lenders, doctors and merchants were allowed into the city by day, but were compelled by law to return to the ghetto at night and on Christian holidays. (The word 'ghetto' means a district of a city occupied by a minority group.) While Shakespeare does not use the word 'ghetto', it can be helpful to think about how these different districts – and experiences of Venetian life – might be conveyed on stage. The Jewish ghetto in Venice (Cannaregio) can still be visited today.

BELMONT

The action of the play moves between a real place, Venice, and the fictional Belmont. Shakespeare contrasts the two settings: while Venice is a city, Portia's house in Belmont is set some distance away from this busy commercial hub. This idea reflects the fact that wealthy people in Shakespeare's time had a home in London (used when they had business at Court) and a country estate. Women would often have remained in the country when their husbands went to London and this helps to account for the idea that Belmont is very much run by a woman.

KEY CONTEXT (A03)

Many of Shakespeare's plays – among them several comedies – have Italian settings. These include *The Taming of the Shrew* (Padua), *The Two Gentleman of Verona* (Verona) and *Much Ado About Nothing* (Messina in Sicily).

TOP TIP: ENGLISH ATTITUDES TO ITALY (A03)

By mixing the familiar and the exotic in his depiction of settings, Shakespeare draws parallels for his Elizabethan audience with their own ways of life, while also appealing to their interest in Italian stories and locations. For English people living on their northern European island, the continent – and the land we know today as Italy – held a great fascination. Italy was seen as a fashion centre and, largely because of its Roman history, as a centre of culture. At this time in England, only the wealthy had baths, and then perhaps only once a year, and it was considered normal to be stitched into your clothes for the winter. Compared to England, the regions of Italy were viewed as stylish and rather intriguing places.

PROGRESS AND REVISION CHECK

SECTION ONE: CHECK YOUR KNOWLEDGE

Answer these quick questions to test your basic knowledge of the themes, contexts and settings of the play:

1 What is the currency of Venice?

2 Who is described by Nerissa as being 'ever virtuous' and 'holy'?

3 Who are Monsieur Le Bon and the County Palatine?

4 Where does Shylock arrange to meet Tubal at the end of Act III Scene 1?

5 What kind of place is the 'Rialto'?

6 Who says 'Good sir, this ring was given me by my wife' and to which theme does this quotation most closely relate?

7 'We do pray for _____,/And that same prayer doth teach us all to render/The deeds of _____.' Which one word is missing here?

8 Who leaves Shylock's service saying 'I am a Jew if I serve the Jew any longer'?

9 Who says 'if you wrong us, shall we not revenge?'?

10 Why does Bassanio mention Tripolis, Mexico, England, Lisbon, Barbary and India in Act III Scene 2?

SECTION TWO: CHECK YOUR UNDERSTANDING

Task: Explain how Shakespeare presents marriage in *The Merchant of Venice*.

Think about:

- the importance of marriage in the play
- how different attitudes to this theme are presented.

> **TOP TIP** (A01)
>
> This task requires more thought and a slightly longer response. Try to write at least three to four paragraphs.

PROGRESS CHECK

GOOD PROGRESS

I can:

- explain the main themes, contexts and settings in the text and how they contribute to the effect on the reader ☐
- use a range of appropriate evidence to support any points I make about these elements. ☐

EXCELLENT PROGRESS

I can:

- analyse in detail the way themes are developed and presented across the play ☐
- refer closely to key aspects of context and setting and the implications they have for the writer's viewpoint, and the interpretation of relationships and ideas. ☐

FORM

OVERVIEW

Like all of Shakespeare's plays, *The Merchant of Venice* is a play in five acts, with each act divided into scenes. In terms of genre, the play fulfils the criteria for a comedy; however, the intolerance shown towards Shylock casts a shadow over the play's concluding scenes.

SHAKESPEAREAN COMEDY

Shakespeare's comedies are light-hearted plays with happy endings that involve marriages, reunions and other kinds of gathering. Other famous Shakespearean comedies include *As You Like It*, *Much Ado About Nothing*, *A Midsummer Night's Dream* and *The Taming of the Shrew*. By the end of a comedy, problems are solved happily and disaster – in this case, the loss of Antonio's life – is averted. The play's multiple marriages and the spirit of friendship between these characters also add to an atmosphere of celebration.

TRAGIC EVENTS

Although the play is not classified as a tragedy, there is a note of tragedy in Shylock's downfall and in the pathos and pity of modern audiences' reactions to him. Another common feature of Shakespearean tragedy is eloquent speeches that give us insights into a character's state of mind. Shylock does not have soliloquies, but he does speak with great passion and humanity about the treatment of Jews.

TOP TIP: BREAKING TENSION WITH COMEDY

As with many of Shakespeare's plays of any genre, there are occasional breaks in the tension for audience-pleasing humour. The use of comic characters such as the Gobbos, Morocco, Arragon and, to some extent, Gratiano, is very important at key points in a drama to relax the tension and allow it to be built up again to a higher level in the scenes that follow, creating interesting juxtapositions between characters, situations and locations. We know that Elizabethan theatre-goers enjoyed foolish antics, wordplay and watching pompous or boastful characters cut down to size, and it is interesting to consider how the comic element of scenes such as Act II Scene 2 and Act III Scene 5 might be staged.

STRUCTURE

OVERVIEW

The Merchant of Venice combines several plots. It is useful to think about how Shakespeare uses moods, themes and motifs at various points in the play to draw parallels and contrasts between some of these different elements. These moods, themes and motifs include sadness, loyalty, the bond, the test, money, and parent/child relationships. Techniques such as these unify the play as a satisfying dramatic experience for audiences.

STORYLINES

The play has a number of plot strands: the two principal ones involve Antonio and Shylock's bond and the 'pound of flesh' (IV.1.230) (Acts I–IV, set in Venice) and Portia and the caskets (Acts I–III, set in Belmont). The story of Jessica and Lorenzo's elopement and its consequences runs from Act II to Act V, and the story involving Portia, Bassanio, Nerissa, Gratiano and the rings used as a test of loyalty runs from Act IV into Act V. Shakespeare weaves the different plots together, never spending so much time on one that we forget about the others. Sometimes the audience is ahead of the characters, such as in the episode with the rings. On other occasions the audience is not shown something until the characters themselves see it, as in the choice of the caskets. By varying the use of these techniques, Shakespeare is able to develop both humour and dramatic tension.

SUSPENSE AND PACE

In *The Merchant of Venice,* Shakespeare creates moments of great suspense. Much of this is done by switching between plots and settings at vital points in the proceedings. For example, in Act I Scene 2 we learn that Portia must marry whichever man chooses the correct casket. At the end of the scene, the arrival of the Prince of Morocco is announced, but we have to wait while Shylock and Antonio agree the bond before we are taken back to Portia. Even then, in Act II Scene 1, we do not see Morocco make his choice; we have to wait until Act II Scene 7 for this. By the time Morocco chooses the gold casket, another plot has been introduced: the planned elopement of Jessica with Lorenzo. It is the ominous rumours about Antonio's ships that create the greatest sense of anxious uncertainty, however, as they escalate from the possibility that Antonio has lost a ship in Act II Scene 8 to Bassanio's 'Hath all his ventures failed?' (III.2.265).

CHECKPOINT 14 (A01)

How many scenes does the play contain?

REVISION FOCUS: ACTS AND SCENES

Make a table or chart to give you an overview of the acts and scenes of the play, and their varying lengths, contents, key characters and settings. You could make a copy of the diagram on the next page and then annotate it. Or create your own version. Notice how Act II moves at a fast pace through nine scenes, many of them short. Likewise, at nineteen lines long, Act IV Scene 2 is also brief: an informal street scene, which contrasts with the tension and formality of the trial, before the action moves back to Belmont in Act V.

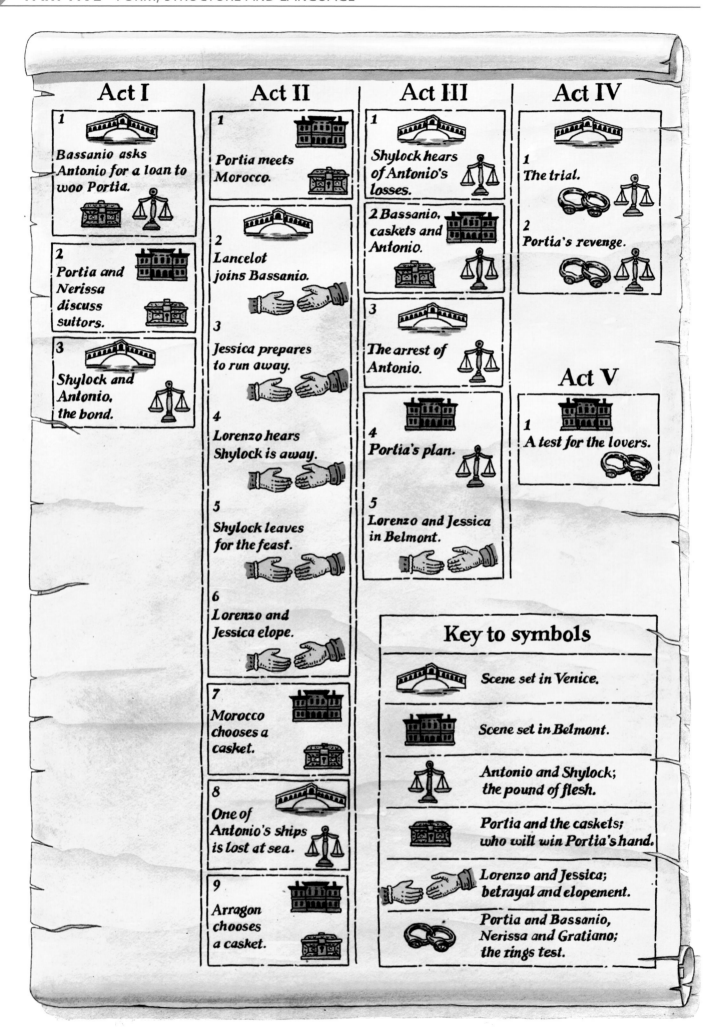

Act I

1 Bassanio asks Antonio for a loan to woo Portia.

2 Portia and Nerissa discuss suitors.

3 Shylock and Antonio, the bond.

Act II

1 Portia meets Morocco.

2 Lancelot joins Bassanio.

3 Jessica prepares to run away.

4 Lorenzo hears Shylock is away.

5 Shylock leaves for the feast.

6 Lorenzo and Jessica elope.

7 Morocco chooses a casket.

8 One of Antonio's ships is lost at sea.

9 Arragon chooses a casket.

Act III

1 Shylock hears of Antonio's losses.

2 Bassanio, caskets and Antonio.

3 The arrest of Antonio.

4 Portia's plan.

5 Lorenzo and Jessica in Belmont.

Act IV

1 The trial.

2 Portia's revenge.

Act V

1 A test for the lovers.

Key to symbols

	Scene set in Venice.
	Scene set in Belmont.
	Antonio and Shylock; the pound of flesh.
	Portia and the caskets; who will win Portia's hand.
	Lorenzo and Jessica; betrayal and elopement.
	Portia and Bassanio, Nerissa and Gratiano; the rings test.

LANGUAGE

OVERVIEW

Shakespeare's language in *The Merchant of Venice* is a rich and varied mixture of blank verse and prose. The playwright uses a range of techniques to create a variety of striking effects to provide us with insights into:

- a character's state of mind at a particular point in the play, e.g. Antonio's melancholy or Shylock's distress
- characters' feelings and intentions towards each other, e.g. to persuade, to insult, to mock.

LANGUAGE DEVICE: BLANK VERSE

What is blank verse?	Blank verse is unrhymed verse in iambic pentameter. It is used more often than rhyming verse in Shakespeare because it is more versatile in that it can create a greater range of effects including more naturalistic ones.
Example	'Have by some surgeon, Shylock, on your charge,/To stop his wounds, lest he do bleed to death.' (Portia, IV.1.255–6)
Effect	Shakespeare uses blank verse in the trial scene because of the formality of the situation, the importance of the characters and the seriousness of what they are speaking about. The only section of this scene to be written in prose is Dr Bellario's letter, which creates an audible contrast for the audience between the text being read aloud and the dialogue of the characters speaking at the trial.

KEY CONTEXT (A03)

Several of Shakespeare's plays involve some kind of trial. By their very nature trials are likely to be serious and formal events whose proceedings create suspense and whose verdicts bring matters to a climax, and Shakespeare's language choices in Act IV Scene 1 reflect this.

LANGUAGE DEVICE: PROSE

What is prose?	Prose does not have line breaks like verse. It sounds less literary and more like 'ordinary' speech than verse.
Example	'If he should offer to choose, and choose the right casket, you should refuse to perform your father's will if you should refuse to accept him.' (I.2.84–6)
Effect	Shakespeare uses prose here to show that Portia and Nerissa are relaxed and are talking relatively casually to each other. Prose can also be used to reflect the lower status of characters, to show mental distress, or for some kinds of comic scene.

REVSION FOCUS: VERSE AND PROSE

Make a note in your text to show whether blank verse or prose is being used and to highlight where Shakespeare shifts from one to the other. Reflect on why you think prose or verse has been chosen and make notes about the range of effects achieved.

LANGUAGE DEVICE: COURTLY LOVE

What is courtly love?	Shakespeare's audiences would have been familiar with the idea of courtly love, and the language associated with it. Lovers were expected to describe one another's finest attributes and virtues in language rich in descriptions, superlatives, exclamations and classical allusions.
Example	'Fair Portia's counterfeit! What demi-god/Hath come so near creation?' (III.2.115–16)
Effect	Such speech shows the depth of feeling between the characters and their levels of excitement. Bassanio uses techniques like hyperbole and a rhetorical question to convey his sentiments here.

TOP TIP (A02)

Look out for other uses of rhetorical questions. Shylock's famous and memorable speech in Act III Scene 1 uses them to powerful effect, for example: 'Hath not a Jew eyes?' (III.1.52) and 'If you prick us, do we not bleed?' (III.1.57).

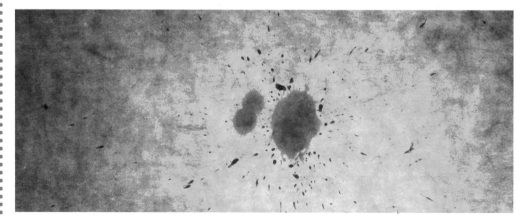

LANGUAGE DEVICE: RIDDLES AND RHYMES

What are riddles and rhymes?	The inscriptions on the scrolls within the three caskets – and the song that is sung while Bassanio is deciding in Act III Scene 2 – sound rather like nursery rhymes or riddles and adopt a playful, even teasing tone.
Example	'All that glisters is not gold;/Often have you heard that told./Many a man his life hath sold/But my outside to behold.' (II.7.65–8)
Effect	The inscriptions have a playful, teasing quality. To establish a contrast with the style of verse used elsewhere, Shakespeare changes the rhythm from iambic pentameter to trochaic tetrameter (a shorter line of four beats in a stressed/unstressed pattern) and from blank verse to rhyming couplets.

TOP TIP   **A02**

Rhyme can also be used for emphasis or to let the audience know that a scene is about to end.

LANGUAGE DEVICE: IMAGERY

What is imagery?	Imagery is vivid and descriptive language that helps the reader to understand and respond to what a character says.
Example	'The quality of mercy is not strain'd,/It droppeth as the gentle rain from heaven/Upon the place beneath.' (IV.1.182–4)
Effect	Portia's simile here uses a concrete image (rain) to help the courtroom of listeners understand something abstract (mercy). Much of the power of this image lies in the way that it connects the heavenly and the earthly, and in the way the gentle sounds of the words reflect what she is trying to say about gentleness.

KEY QUOTATION: 'I WOULD HAVE MY BOND'   **A02**

In Act IV Scene 1 Shylock repeats the same phrase, 'I would have my bond' (IV.1.87). This shows he is preoccupied to the point of obsession with the idea of revenge. Can you find other examples in this play where Shakespeare uses repetition to show us the intensity of a character's feelings?

LANGUAGE DEVICE: PUNS AND MALAPROPISMS

CHECKPOINT 15 (A01)

Which character is irritatingly talkative in Act I Scene 1?

What are puns and malapropisms?	A **pun** is a form of wordplay that exploits the fact that certain words sound alike. The word **malapropism** is used when someone mistakenly confuses words.
Example	Pun: 'It is much that the <u>Moor</u> should be <u>more</u> than reason; but if she be less than an honest woman, she is indeed <u>more</u> than I took her for.' (III.5.35–7) Malapropism: 'I was always plain with you, and so now I speak my <u>agitation</u> of the matter.' (III.5.3–4)
Effect	With such wordplay, Shakespeare establishes Lancelot Gobbo as a comic character – the play's 'fool'. Some of the humour derives from Lancelot trying to use clever words, but failing (for example saying 'agitation' – excitement/anxiety – when he means 'cogitation' – thoughts). This conveys to the audience that he would like to better himself and climb up the social ladder but that he is unlikely to be very successful.

LANGUAGE DEVICE: OXYMORONS

TOP TIP (A02)

Rhyme can also be used for emphasis or to let the audience know that a scene is about to end.

What is an oxymoron?	An **oxymoron** is a figure of speech that combines words that seem to contradict each other.
Example	Bassanio cries 'O happy torment' in Act III Scene 2 line 37.
Effect	Bassanio's use of the words 'happy' and 'torment' together reflects his understanding that Portia is both the source of his torment and the person who can release him from it.

REVISION FOCUS: QUOTATIONS

Keep a record of key quotations by selecting important ones and recording them in a little notebook or on a note-making app on your phone or laptop. Alternatively make a set of quotation cards or slides and look at them regularly to help you memorise them.

PROGRESS AND REVISION CHECK

SECTION ONE: CHECK YOUR KNOWLEDGE

Answer these quick questions to test your basic knowledge of the form, structure and language of the play:

1 Which is the first scene to be set in Belmont?

2 Name two characters who speak in verse in Act II Scene 2.

3 What language technique is used in: 'Come on, in this there can be no dismay,/My ships come home a month before the day.' (I.3.176–7)

4 What do all the following words from the play have in common: 'knell', 'carrion', 'tombs', 'halter', 'gallows'?

5 Complete the following rhetorical question: 'If you _____ us, do we not die?' (III.1.58–9)

6 What does Portia mean by calling Falconbridge a 'dumbshow' (I.2.67–8) and the Duke of Saxony's nephew a 'sponge' (I.2.91)?

7 What device is 'the devil incarnation' (II.2.24) an example of?

8 Why does the letter that Bassanio opens in Act III Scene 2 completely change the mood of the scene?

9 What do the following words from the play have in common: 'sentence', 'judgement', 'decrees', 'court', 'plea'?

10 Which word is repeated in Act V Scene 1 lines 192–208 for comic effect?

SECTION TWO: CHECK YOUR UNDERSTANDING

Task: To what extent would you describe *The Merchant of Venice* as a comedy?

Think about:

- the play's storyline and structure
- the use of humour in the play, and how this is created.

> **TOP TIP** **A01**
>
> This task requires more thought and a slightly longer response. Try to write at least three to four paragraphs.

PROGRESS CHECK

GOOD PROGRESS

I can:

- explain how Shakepeare uses form, structure and language to develop the action, show relationships and develop ideas. ☐
- use relevant quotations to support the points I make, and make reference to the effect of some language choices. ☐

EXCELLENT PROGRESS

I can:

- analyse in detail Shakespeare's use of particular forms, structures and language techniques to convey ideas, create characters and evoke mood or setting. ☐
- select from a range of evidence, including apt quotations, to infer the effect of particular language choices and to develop wider interpretations. ☐

UNDERSTANDING THE QUESTION

For your exam, you will be answering an extract-based question and/or a question on the whole of *The Merchant of Venice*. Check with your teacher to see what sort of question you are doing. Whatever the task, questions in exams will need **decoding**. This means highlighting and understanding the key words so that the answer you write is relevant.

BREAK DOWN THE QUESTION

Pick out the **key words** or phrases. For example:

Read the text from Act IV Scene 1, 'A pound of that same merchant's flesh is thine' to 'He shall have merely justice and his bond.' (lines 297–337)

Question: How does Shakespeare **present attitudes** towards **the law and justice** in **this extract** and in the **play as a whole**?

What does this tell you?

● Focus on the **themes** of the **law** and **justice** but also on **'attitudes'** – so **different characters'** views on them.

● The word **'present'** tells you that you should focus on the ways Shakespeare reveals these attitudes, i.e. the **techniques** he uses.

● The phrases 'this extract' and 'play as a whole' mean you need to **start** with the given **extract** and then **widen your discussion** to the rest of the play, but stick to the theme in **both**.

PLANNING YOUR ANSWER

It is vital that you generate ideas quickly and plan your answer efficiently when you sit the exam. Stick to your plan and, with a watch at your side, tick off each part as you progress.

STAGE 1: GENERATE IDEAS QUICKLY

Briefly **list your key ideas** based on the question you have **decoded**. For example:

In the **extract**:

● *Portia declares that the bond is legally binding and the court must respect Shylock's right to take his pound of flesh.*

● *Shylock praises the lawyer's good sense and judgement.*

● *Portia wins the case on a technicality – no blood can be spilled in taking a pound of flesh.*

In the **play as a whole**:

● *Jewish Venetians had fewer rights than Christians at the time.*

● *Antonio's treatment of Shylock in the past has been disrespectful but Shylock could not retaliate.*

● *In Act III Scene 4 Portia plans to defend her husband's friend disguised as a man; this would not have been possible as a woman.*

TOP TIP (A02)

When discussing Shakespeare's language, make sure you refer to the techniques he uses and, most importantly, the *effect* of those techniques. Don't just write: *Shakespeare writes in verse here*; write: *Shakespeare's use of blank verse shows/ demonstrates/ conveys … .*

STAGE 2: JOT DOWN USEFUL QUOTATIONS (OR KEY EVENTS)

For example, from the **extract**: 'Shed thou no blood, nor cut thou less nor more/But just a pound of flesh' (lines 323–4)

From the **play as a whole**: 'use thou all th'endeavour of a man/In speed to Padua' (III.4.48–9)

STAGE 3: PLAN FOR PARAGRAPHS

Use paragraphs to plan your answer. For example:

Paragraph	Point
Paragraph 1	**Introduce** the **argument** you wish to make: *Shakespeare explores the themes of law and justice in this climactic scene and throughout the play. This extract from Act IV Scene 1 clearly shows how Shylock feels empowered and believes the law to be working in his favour but by the end of the extract it is clear that this is not the case.*
Paragraph 2	Your first point: *Portia asserts that the bond is upheld by the court: 'The law allows it, and the court awards it.' Shylock repeatedly praises the lawyer's good sense and judgement, showing his confidence and sense of empowerment at this point.*
Paragraph 3	Your second point: *However, by the end of this extract, Portia explains that Shylock may only take flesh but no blood and that the amount Shylock takes must be exact. The impossibility of this stops Shylock's revenge on Antonio in its tracks, and the change in his circumstances is instantaneous. As Gratiano puts it, 'Now, infidel, I have you on the hip.'*
Paragraph 4	Your third point: *Gratiano's comment is a reminder of how Jews were widely viewed in Venice and elsewhere at this time, and this was enshrined in Venetian law by decree. We learn about how Antonio has treated Shylock in the past in Act I Scene 3 and it is clear that the 'bond' is purely a financial transaction and that Antonio still views him as an 'enemy'.*
Paragraph 5	Your fourth point: *Shakespeare shows the audience that the Venetian concept of 'justice' is unfair to Jews. Portia's need to disguise herself is another reminder of how society gives people different status based on religion, race and gender.*
Conclusion	**Sum up** your argument: *This scene – set in a courtroom and presided over by the Duke of Venice – is central to Shakespeare's exploration of the themes of law and justice in the play. Portia speaks movingly about 'mercy' but the treatment of Jews by Venetian society continues to be merciless.*

TOP TIP

You may not have time to write such a detailed plan in the exam, but this is a good example of how to structure your ideas into paragraphs. Remember to back up your points with evidence from the text, events or quotations.

RESPONDING TO WRITERS' EFFECTS

The two most important assessment objectives are **AO1** and **AO2**. They are about *what* writers do (the choices they make, and the effects these create), *what* your ideas are (your analysis and interpretation) and *how* you write about them (how well you explain your ideas).

ASSESSMENT OBJECTIVE 1 (AO1)

What does it say?	What does it mean?	Dos and don'ts
Read, understand and respond to texts. Students should be able to: ● Maintain a critical style and develop an informed personal response ● Use textual references, including quotations, to support and illustrate interpretations	You must: ● Use some of the literary terms you have learned (correctly!) ● Write in a professional way (not a sloppy, chatty way) ● Show that you have thought for yourself ● Back up your ideas with examples, including quotations	**Don't write …** *Jessica seems to really hate her father and can't wait to run off with her boyfriend.* **Do write …** *Jessica is shown to be unhappy at home with Shylock and desperate to elope with Lorenzo. At the end of Act II Scene 5, she says 'I have a father, you a daughter, lost' showing that she is aware of the finality and seriousness of her decision.*

IMPROVING YOUR CRITICAL STYLE

Use a variety of words and phrases to show effects:

Shakespeare *suggests …, conveys …, implies …, presents how …, explores …, demonstrates …, describes how …, shows how …*
I/we (as readers) *infer …, recognise …, understand …, question …, see …, are given …, reflect …*

For example, look at these two alternative paragraphs by different students about Bassanio. Note the difference in the quality of expression.

Student A:

> Retelling story rather than critical

Bassanio was Antonio's best friend so he went so see Antonio to borrow more money. He talks about an arrow saying that he will shoot another arrow in the same direction. This shows that he was feeling good about paying back everything he owes. This shows he doesn't mind risks.

> Chatty and informal, uses past instead of present tense

> Unclear whether 'He' refers to Bassanio or Antonio

> Repetitive – better to use an alternative

Student B:

Makes it clear that Bassanio is a literary construct

Clear and precise language

Phrase allows the student to explore the idea rather than state it as fact

Shakespeare presents Bassanio as youthful and optimistic when he visits Antonio in the play's opening scene. Shakespeare shows the audience that Antonio is well aware of Bassanio's profligate past. The verbs 'unburden' and 'get clear' imply that Bassanio is being honest with Antonio but also that he is dependent on Antonio's help. Shakespeare also seems to be suggesting that because Antonio has given Bassanio both love and money, they have almost become one and the same thing.

Clear and precise language

Variety of critical phrases

Looks beyond the obvious and infers meaning with personal interpretation

ASSESSMENT OBJECTIVE 2 (A02)

What does it say?	What does it mean?	Dos and don'ts
Analyse the language, form and structure used by the writer to create meanings and effects, using relevant subject terminology where appropriate.	'Analyse' – comment **in detail** on **particular aspects** of the text or language. 'language' – vocabulary, imagery, metre, etc. 'form' – **how** the story is told (e.g. five act play, dramatic genre and its conventions) 'structure' – the **order** in which events are revealed, or in which characters appear, or descriptions are presented 'create meanings' – what can we, as readers, **infer** from what the writer tells us? What is **implied** by particular descriptions, or events? 'subject terminology' – **words** you should use when writing about plays, such as 'act' 'scene', 'stage direction', etc.	**Don't write:** *Portia doesn't like her suitors.* **Do write:** *Shakespeare's language choices convey Portia's disdain for her various suitors. She mocks them using words like 'colt' and 'sponge' and uses exclamations to show the strength of her feeling: 'God defend me from these two!' and 'How oddly he is suited!' The audience only knows about these young men courtesy of Portia's dismissive but highly entertaining descriptions.*

IMPLICATIONS, INFERENCES AND INTERPRETATIONS

- The best analysis focuses on specific ideas or events, or uses of language and thinks about what is implied.
- This means drawing inferences. On the surface, Portia tells Bassanio her husband will be her 'lord' and everything she has will be his. But how does some of her language and behaviour challenge conventional ideas about the role and status of women in society?
- From the inferences you make across the text as a whole, you can arrive at your own interpretation – a sense of the bigger picture, a wider evaluation of a character, relationship or idea.

USING QUOTATIONS

One of the secrets of success in writing exam essays is to use quotations **effectively**. There are five basic principles:

1. Only quote what is most useful.
2. Do not use a quotation that repeats what you have just written.
3. Put quotation marks, e.g. ' ', around the quotation.
4. Write the quotation exactly as it appears in the original.
5. Use the quotation so that it fits neatly into your sentence.

EXAM FOCUS: USING QUOTATIONS (A01)

Quotations should be used to develop the line of thought in your essay, and to 'zoom in' on key details, such as language choices. The mid-level response below shows a clear and effective way of doing this:

| Makes a clear point |
| Gives an apt quotation, embedded well |

Shakespeare presents Morocco as a boastful man. In Act II Scene I, Morocco says he would 'mock the lion' to win Portia. Shakespeare shows the reader that Morocco likes to exaggerate things.

| Explains the effect of the quotation |

However, **high-level responses** will go even further. They will make an even more precise point, support it with an even more appropriate quotation, focus in on particular words or phrases, and explain the effect or what is implied to make a wider point or draw inferences. Here is an example:

| Precise point |

Shakespeare presents Morocco as a rather boastful man who believes that even if he is unlucky, he will have lost out to an 'unworthier' man. He gives a long list of the things he would do for Portia, including that he would 'Pluck the young sucking cubs from the she-bear,/ ... To win thee'. The use of hyperbole and the

| Precise quotation |

| Language features |

ostentatious use of assonance and onomatopoeia convey to the reader that Morocco is given to melodrama and exaggeration and that he is rather self-important. The impact of this on an audience might be to make them feel sympathy with Portia since, if Act I Scene 2 is anything to go by, Morocco is just one in a long

| Explanation/ implication/effect |

| Further development/link |

list of insufferable suitors and tension builds as his casket test approaches.

SPELLING, PUNCTUATION AND GRAMMAR

SPELLING

Remember to spell correctly the **author's** name, the names of all the **characters**, and the names of **places**.

PUNCTUATION

Remember:

- Use full stops and commas in sentences accurately to make clear points. Don't write long, rambling sentences that don't make sense; equally, avoid using a lot of short repetitive ones. Write in a fluent way, using linking words and phrases.

Don't write	Do write
Nerissa and Portia have a conversation about her father and his will and why anyone who marries her has to choose the correct casket and say they will never marry.	*Nerissa and Portia discuss the details of Portia's late father's will. In order to marry Portia, a suitor must choose the correct casket. If unsuccessful, he must vow never to marry.*

TOP TIP: PRACTICE MAKES PERFECT (A04)

Practise your spellings of key literary terms you might use when writing about the text such as: simile, metaphor, oxymoron, imagery, heroic, villainous, tragedy, etc.

GRAMMAR

When you are writing about the text, make sure you:

- Use the present tense for discussing what the writer does, e.g. *Shakespeare presents …*
- Vary character names with pronouns and use references back to make your writing flow.

Don't write	Do write
Portia and Nerissa were having fun at Bassanio and Gratiano's expense. Portia and Nerissa said that the rings should never have been given away. Bassanio and Gratiano tried to explain how they came to give away their rings but they didn't really succeed.	*Portia and Nerissa amuse themselves at their husbands' expense. They scold Bassanio and Gratiano for parting with the rings. The husbands try to explain their actions, but to no avail.*

TOP TIP (A04)

Even if spelling, punctuation and grammar are not formally assessed by your exam board/ awarding body for this text (e.g. Edexcel), it is still important to ensure that you write accurately and clearly in order to get your points across to the examiner in the best possible way.

TOP TIP (A04)

Enliven your essay by varying the way your sentences begin. For example, *Antonio's sensitivity and generosity towards Bassanio contrast with his harsh treatment of Shylock* can also be written as: *In contrast to his harsh treatment of Shylock, Antonio is sensitive and generous towards Bassanio.*

ANNOTATED SAMPLE ANSWERS

This section provides three **sample responses**, one at a **mid** level, one at a **good** level, and one at a **very high** level.

> **Question:** In Act II Scene 3, Jessica speaks with Lancelot Gobbo and gives him a letter to pass to her lover, Lorenzo.
>
> Starting with this scene, write about how Shakespeare presents Jessica and her relationship with her father Shylock.
>
> Write about how Shakespeare presents Jessica and her relationship with Shylock:
>
> - in this scene
> - elsewhere in the play.

SAMPLE ANSWER 1

A02 Brief reference to form and structure, not developed

This is a very short scene where Jessica speaks to Lancelot who is leaving Shylock's house and she gives him some money. She also asks him to give Lorenzo a letter because he is a guest of 'thy new master' meaning Bassanio. Lancelot says 'Adieu' to Jessica and they both seem sad about parting. After he has gone, Jessica talks more about her father and about Lorenzo and her relationships with them.

A04 Long opening sentence

A01 Well integrated quotations, but not strictly relevant to question

A01 Interesting explanation of text, could be explained further

Jessica is called 'beautiful' and 'sweet' by Lancelot. She is behaving secretively from her father Shylock because she finds her house is like 'hell' and she wants to be with her lover. She does seem a bit torn between them though because she thinks it is a 'sin .../To be asham'd to be my father's child!' She says she is related in 'blood' only but not in 'manners'. This links to the idea that she will marry Lorenzo and become a Christian later in the play.

A02 Clear link to other events in play, needs further language analysis

A01 Insightful point, though expression should be more formal

Her acting 'secretly' links to the secret letter to Lorenzo and also the fact that she will be meeting her new husband in disguise. This reminds me of 'Romeo and Juliet' where the lovers come from different families and meet at a party in disguise. Jessica dresses up as a boy to make her escape. Lorenzo says to her 'So are you, sweet,/Even in the lovely garnish of a boy.' Jessica is dressing and behaving with more freedom and is shown love by Lorenzo. I think this is different from her dull life with Shylock.

A03 Interesting connection but not developed

A03 Relevant point about context

A02 Opportunity to discuss dramatic irony here

We see Shylock and Jessica together in Act II Scene 5. In contrast to what we know she is about to do, he calls the revellers 'Christian fools'. This could connect to the fact that Jews in Venice at this time were not allowed outside their ghetto after a particular time and on special dates in the Christian calendar. He says his house is 'sober' and he seems proud that his family does not enjoy 'shallow foppery' like Bassanio and the others. He doesn't realise that his daughter is going to join the masquers. I think their relationship is that he is very strict with her.

A01 Personal view but too simply expressed

We learn that Jessica has strong feelings for Lorenzo in this scene. In Act II Scene 6 Jessica calls him 'my love' and Lorenzo praises her using the adjectives 'wise, fair, and true'. Jessica has been brave to run off with Lorenzo and we see this escape happen in Act II and how Shylock reacts in Act III. Shakespeare uses lots of short scenes in Act II to show that things are happening quickly. Then in Act III we see that Jessica leaving Shylock has had a big impact on him. He is shocked and angry that she has taken his money. I think this is when he really starts to want revenge.

A02 Analyses language used, but not effect

A01 Needs a stronger conclusion with reference to the relationship

MID LEVEL

Comment
Some good points about Jessica and Shylock although the answer could have focused more sharply and consistently on the father/daughter relationship as the question asks. There is some reference to other scenes but evidence could be more wide-ranging. Useful reference to context. More thorough analysis of author's methods required.

For a Good Level:
- Aim for a more fluent writing style with more explanations of meanings.
- Make greater reference to the effects of language, structure and form.
- Select a wider range of examples from elsewhere in the play.
- Construct a clearer line of argument in direct response to the question.

SAMPLE ANSWER 2

A01 Clear, confident opening

Act II is a fast-paced section of Shakespeare's play. Jessica is an important character in this section and this is the first time the audience sees her. Shakespeare establishes her as a kind character and Lancelot seems loyal to her. There is a parallel here as both will leave Shylock's household, looking for better prospects. They will both be entering Christian households and hope for a more prosperous and happy life.

A04 Link fluently expressed

In this scene, Jessica says her father's house is 'hell' and that it has a 'taste of tediousness'. She says that Lancelot's fooling helped her to be less bored. She calls Lancelot Gobbo 'a merry devil' and this description implies that life with Shylock is simple and sober. When left alone on stage at the end of this short scene, Jessica exclaims 'what a heinous sin it is in me/ To be asham'd to be my father's child!' Her home is a hell to her because of her father's behaviour but also her guilt at having such negative feelings towards her Jewish father, whom she feels she should respect and obey. This contrasts with the party atmosphere later in Act II. We know from Act II Scene 5 that Shylock seems to despise the masques and those who enjoy them with their 'varnish'd faces'. Shylock has 'no mind of feasting' although we know from Act I Scene 3 that he was invited to dine with them by Bassanio.

A02 Analysis of language and what it implies

A01 Point is argued confidently here, secure knowledge of text

A01 Links ideas fluently

A01 A general statement, losing focus on Shylock and Jessica here

A01 Clear topic sentence

There are several places in the play where there is conflict and disagreement between generations of a family and between fathers and daughters in particular. Portia struggles with the fact that she feels 'curbed' by the will of her late father, although she does not go against his wishes.

A01 Interesting point, well made

Jessica however is seen to be putting her escape plan in motion in this scene. She passes Lancelot a letter for Lorenzo. In the scene that follows, Lorenzo is making plans and the letter arrives. Lorenzo speaks tenderly about Jessica and praises her virtues: 'whiter than the paper it writ on/Is the fair hand that writ'. This conveys the idea that their love for each other is sincere, and reflects ideas of the time about what a woman's virtues should be, such as modesty, purity and beauty. This contrasts with how Shylock will describe her when he hears she has gone and taken many of his riches with her. While he lovingly describes his jewels as 'precious, precious', his language about Jessica is extremely bitter. He

A01 Narrative detail not needed here

A03 Relevant and insightful point about context

A02 — Precise comment about the tone of Shylock's language in this speech

repeatedly calls her a 'thief' and wishes she were 'dead at my foot' and 'hearsed' with 'the ducats in her coffin'. This morbid language shows us that Shylock views her actions as unforgiveable and strongly implies that she is worthless to him now, as he wishes her dead. Despite their differences, it is interesting that Shakespeare draws a parallel between father and daughter in that they both suffer feelings of resentment and shame because of the attitude and behaviour of the other.

A01 — Useful comparison summing up the relationship

GOOD LEVEL

Comment

The text is interpreted thoughtfully in some detail and there is textual evidence to support points although analysis of this evidence could explore effects of language further, and consider different possible meanings. The candidate has good textual and contextual knowledge and has a clear sense of Jessica's importance as a character beyond this scene. A more confident answer might have considered some of the themes and issues raised in more depth.

For a High Level:

- Develop a clearer and more confident overall line of argument.
- Make more links between close analysis and wider themes, concepts, etc.
- Demonstrate even more of a sense of the author at work and consider intended effects on audience.
- Could make more use of contextual knowledge in places.

SAMPLE ANSWER 3

A01 Argues point powerfully and precisely

In this scene, Shylock's daughter Jessica prepares to escape from Shylock's house. Although this is the first time the audience sees Jessica, her words in this scene and the urgency with which she seeks to leave the household convey her unhappiness and imply that her relationship with her father is under strain. Jessica's language suggests that her life with her father has been a form of torture, by using the word 'hell'. This develops the theological language ('conscience', 'fiend') that Lancelot uses (and misuses) in the previous scene. It also foreshadows not only her desertion of her family home but also her conversion to a new faith and contributes to the prevailing view of Shylock as un-Christian both literally and metaphorically in his treatment of others.

A02 Subtle comments about language

A02 Excellent structural point

The audience sees almost nothing of Shylock's life and lifestyle for themselves, relying on reports and hearsay from other characters. We do however see Shylock and Jessica together in Act II Scene 5 and it is perhaps telling that Jessica says very little in his presence here. We may even gain an impression of Shylock as a despotic father, repeatedly calling for his daughter, giving her orders: 'Look to my house', 'Hear you me, Jessica', 'Do as I bid you' and firm advice: 'Fast bind, fast find:/A proverb never stale in thrifty mind.' Alternatively this language could be interpreted and performed on stage as over-protective yet well-meaning, and would certainly not have seemed alien to an Elizabethan audience aware of duty and loyalty owed to parents by children.

A01 Apt quotations, well embedded

A01 High-level discussion of different possible meanings

A03 Perceptive ideas developed by placing text in a fresh context

Another way to consider Shakespeare's presentation of Shylock and Jessica is to view the strain on their relationship as being linked to youth and age, and to differing cultural attitudes to pleasure and parties. In this way, Shakespeare's portrayal of Shylock at this point in the play may have something in common with the puritanical Malvolio from another Shakespearean comedy 'Twelfth Night'. Elizabethan audiences might have heard in Shylock's reaction to the masque a note of puritan disdain for frivolity and feasting. For example, when Shylock describes 'the vile squealing of the wry-neck'd fife' (a small musical instrument), this conveys an impression of Shylock as snobbish and humourless, whereas the audience will be on Jessica's side when she transgresses by leaving home, wearing a man's clothing, and converting to a new faith. This suggests that Shakespeare uses the relationship between father and daughter to explore differences in cultural attitudes, not only between the generation, but between different sections of society and faiths.

By the end of Act II, Jessica has made her escape dressed as a male torchbearer. Shakespeare develops the themes of secrecy and of appearances being misleading here, with Jessica saying in Act II Scene 6 that holding a torch is 'an office of discovery .../And I should be obscur'd'. Her choice of the word 'obscur'd' is an example of enjoyable wordplay but also hints at her mental anguish – it is almost as if she feels cloaked in shame, a word she also used in Act II Scene 3 to describe her feelings towards her father. Her emotions, throughout this series of scenes in which her world changes forever, are understandably ambivalent. In order to be true to herself and her principles, she has had to use secrecy and deception, and to cast off her identity as a Jew.

(A01) Clever linking of language analysis to broader themes and point about character

Lorenzo and Lancelot Gobbo's words help to build an impression of Jessica as a virtuous woman placed under insufferable strain. Later in the play, on hearing that she has absconded, Shylock will condemn her: 'She is damned for it'. Shylock feels deeply hurt and betrayed and his reaction is shocking, bitter and vengeful. We hear in Act III that Jessica has taken many of Shylock's riches with her and that she has begun to spend them on just the kind of fripperies that will appal her father. However, Shylock's confusion in mourning his loss, 'My daughter! O my ducats! O my daughter!', in a single breath makes him a figure more to be mocked rather than sympathised with. His words may not be seen so much as touching but as evidence that he is irredeemably out of touch with his daughter and her real worth.

(A01) Fluent and elegant writing style

(A01) One of several links to other parts of play

(A01) Strong conclusion focusing on their failed relationship

VERY HIGH LEVEL

Comment

This answer is very convincing and makes interesting connections. The style is fluent and elegant and the overall argument is clear. Paragraphs extend ideas confidently and perceptively. The answer analyses Shakespeare's methods in terms of language, form and structure, and quotations are integrated well into the answer. Relevant contextual information is also skilfully blended into the overall argument.

PRACTICE TASK

Write a full-length response to this exam-style question and then use the **Mark scheme** on page 88 to assess your own response.

> **Question:** In Act II Scene 8, Solanio and Salarino report Shylock's reaction to his daughter's disappearance and the news that one of Antonio's ships could be in trouble.
>
> Read from line 12 ('I never heard a passion so confus'd') to the end of the scene ('With some delight or other.')
>
> Starting with this extract, how does Shakespeare present the theme of money in the play?
>
> Write about how Shakespeare presents the theme of money in:
>
> - this extract
> - the play as a whole.

TOP TIP (A01)

You can use the General skills section of the **Mark scheme** on page 88 to remind you of the key criteria you'll need to cover.

Remember:

- Plan quickly and efficiently by using key words from the question.
- Write equally about the extract and the rest of the play.
- Focus on the techniques Shakespeare uses and the effect of these on the reader.
- Support your ideas with relevant evidence, including quotations.

FURTHER QUESTIONS

1. Explain how Shakespeare explores the theme of loyalty in Act V Scene 1 and elsewhere in the play.

2. Write about the importance of the idea of 'looking beyond appearances' in *The Merchant of Venice*.

3. 'I think he only loves the world for him' (Solanio, II.8.51). How does Shakespeare present the relationship between Bassanio and Antonio in the opening scene and in the play as a whole?

LITERARY TERMS

alliteration	where a sound is repeated at the beginning (or on the stressed syllables) of multiple words to create particular effects
allusion	an indirect reference to something, e.g. another text
aside	where characters speak freely as if other characters cannot hear them
atmosphere	a setting's or situation's mood
backstory	a character's history or background before the text begins
blank verse	unrhymed iambic pentameter
comedy	a light-hearted play in which key characters triumph over adversity
commedia dell'arte	a popular style of professional drama that emerged in northern Italy in the sixteenth century featuring improvisation and recognisable types of characters
courtly love	idealised and devoted love between a knight and a noblewoman, as described in much literature of the Middle Ages
diction	the kind of language in which a text, or section of text, is written, e.g. simple, poetic
dramatic irony	when the audience or reader is aware of something the character is not
fool	a recurring character type in Shakespeare's plays, usually an ignorant clown or a courtly jester
foreshadow	when an author hints at what is to come
genre	a type or style of literature, e.g. comedy or tragedy
hyperbole	exaggerated and extravagant statements
iambic pentameter	a metre where each line is made up of five iambs. An iamb is an unstressed syllable followed by a stressed syllable.
imagery	creating a word picture; common forms are metaphors and similes
juxtaposition	contrast between two things (e.g. scenes) placed close to each other
malaproprism	saying one thing while meaning another, often through understatement, concealment or indirect statement
masque	a form of courtly entertainment that included dancing, dialogue and music
metre	basic rhythmic structure of poetry
morality play	popular kind of drama in fifteenth and sixteenth centuries, in which a protagonist meets characters who represent abstract qualities such as virtues and vices
motif	an image, idea or situation that recurs throughout the text forming a pattern, e.g. references to 'blood' in this play
oxymoron	a phrase or group of words that contradict each other, e.g. 'dark light'
parallel	something which is similar or corresponds in an interesting way to something else
pathos	a moment that makes us feel pity or sorrow
prose	written as ordinary language without the line breaks and metre of verse
pun	a form of wordplay that exploits the fact that certain words sound alike, e.g. 'gentle' and 'Gentile' (meaning non-Jewish)
repetition	a literary device where a word or phrase is repeated for a particular effect
rhetorical question	a question that is asked in order to emphasise a point rather than to receive an answer
rhyme	words with the same end-sounds, frequently used at the ends of lines of poetry

rhyming couplet	a pair of lines that rhyme, often used to mark the end of a scene
riddle	something phrased in such as way as to tease or perplex the reader or listener
simile	a figure of speech using 'like' or 'as' to make a comparison
soliloquy	when a character speaks directly to the audience as if thinking aloud, revealing their inner thoughts, feelings and intentions
stage direction	an instruction within a play relating to an actor's behaviour, movement or speech, or to the set, sound effects, lighting, etc.
symbolise	to use an image to mean or represent something else, often an idea or emotion
tetrameter	a line of four metrical feet
tragedy	a play involving the suffering and the downfall of its central character
tragic hero	a character who makes an error of judgement that leads to his downfall
tragicomedy	a play or novel displaying both tragic and comic aspects
trochee	a stressed syllable followed by an unstressed syllable
verse	writing arranged as lines of poetry with a regular metre as distinct from prose

CHECKPOINT ANSWERS

CHECKPOINT 1, page 11

Belmont

CHECKPOINT 2, page 15

Three thousand ducats

CHECKPOINT 3, page 19

Money bags

CHECKPOINT 4, page 20

She is in disguise so that she can escape from her father's house unnoticed.

CHECKPOINT 5, page 25

Genoa

CHECKPOINT 6, page 27

hazard

CHECKPOINT 7, page 30

In the courtroom in Venice

CHECKPOINT 8, page 32

The Duke of Venice is speaking to Shylock.

CHECKPOINT 9, page 34

That three of Antonio's ships are safe

CHECKPOINT 10, page 42

The Duke of Venice

CHECKPOINT 11, page 44

The letter Salerio brings him with bad news about Antonio

CHECKPOINT 12, page 52

He doesn't charge interest, whereas this is how Shylock makes a living.

CHECKPOINT 13, page 54

Shylock uses these words to describe Balthazar (Portia in disguise).

CHECKPOINT 14, page 63

Twenty

CHECKPOINT 15, page 68

Gratiano

PROGRESS AND REVISION CHECK ANSWERS

PART TWO, pages 36–7

SECTION ONE: CHECK YOUR KNOWLEDGE

1 He wishes to become one of Portia's suitors but doesn't have the 'means'.

2 Because of her dead father's will

3 All of his money is currently tied up in his sea ventures.

4 'bond'

5 Lancelot starts to work for Bassanio.

6 Christianity

7 A skull with a scroll in the eye socket

8 A masque

9 Old Gobbo

10 Arragon

11 A merchant ship

12 The portrait of a fool

13 A casket containing some of Shylock's valuables, including money

14 Take an oath

15 The lead one

16 The Duke of Venice

17 Spill any blood or take any more of less than a 'pound of flesh'

18 Weighing scales

19 Their rings

20 Belmont

SECTION TWO: CHECK YOUR UNDERSTANDING

Task 1

- Two of the play's main characters are introduced and we learn something of the nature of their friendship. Bassanio looks to Antonio as a patron and benefactor, whereas Antonio seems very open and vulnerable to Bassanio's requests. The audience might speculate about whether Antonio's feelings for Bassanio are the cause of his sorrow.

- Bassanio speaks to Antonio about his financial situation and refers to his debts. He proposes that seeking out the rich Portia could help him out of difficulty, but that he needs money to go to Belmont. In this way, another major character (Portia) and storyline (her suitors and the caskets) is introduced, and the next scene will introduce us to Portia and her opinion of her suitors.

- The merchant Antonio's fortunes are tied up in ventures and he will need to borrow money to help his friend. This looks forwards to the introduction of Shylock in Act I Scene 3 and the background of hostility and discrimination between Christians such as Antonio and Jews such as Shylock. This will contrast with the warmth, generosity and friendship in this scene.

- There is something exclusive about Antonio and Bassanio's friendship. While other friends are present at the beginning of this scene (Gratiano, Salarino, Solanio), they leave Antonio and Bassanio to speak alone. The themes of loyalty and friendship will recur throughout the play, in the friendships between Portia and Nerissa for example, and in relation to the matter of the rings at the end of the play.

Task 2

- Portia's judgement demonstrates the power of her wit and skill. By disguising herself as a male lawyer, she is able to prove that she is capable of performing brilliantly in the role. She speaks passionately and poetically about mercy and by doing so, she emphasises Shylock's harsh and vengeful tone and tactics. Her rhetorical skill wins more sympathy from the courtroom and from the audience at this crucial point in the play.

- Portia's judgements on the case reach a climax when, having said that the 'bond' is lawful, she adds that no blood must be spilled and no more or less than a 'pound of flesh' may be taken. A parallel could be drawn between this clever legal move and Shylock's description of his treatment by Antonio in Act I Scene 3 where again it is clear that the law of Venice discriminates against him and offers him no protection or rights.

- The effect on Shylock is that he briefly pleads for his 'principal' but his case has unravelled, and he is once again a resigned and disempowered figure.

- By contrast Antonio, who had seemed resigned to his fate – and who had let his friends plead on his behalf – is empowered once more and uses his voice to seal Shylock's fate: even though the Duke has granted a pardon, the settlement that is agreed takes his fortune and even his religion from him.

PART THREE, page 51

SECTION ONE: CHECK YOUR KNOWLEDGE

1 Bassanio

2 Tubal

3 The Prince of Morocco

4 Dr Bellario

5 Solanio

6 Jessica

7 Antonio

8 Bassanio and Gratiano

9 Portia

10 Lancelot's mother and Jessica's mother/ Shylock's wife

SECTION TWO: CHECK YOUR UNDERSTANDING

- Shakespeare portrays Shylock as a sympathetic character to some extent. For example, in Act I Scene 3 we learn about how he has been treated by Antonio and by others, and how Venetian law prevents him from retaliating or seeking protection under the law.

- Shylock's speech in Act III Scene 1 exposes the hatred and intolerance of which he is a victim. Here, it could be argued that Shakespeare portrays him rather more like a tragic hero than a comic villain. Shakespeare often gives speeches to his villains explaining their motivation, but in this case his appeal to a common humanity is a stirring and powerful argument to which modern audiences living in multicultural societies will respond sympathetically.

- In various other ways, Shakespeare portrays Shylock as obsessed with taking his revenge, for example the repetition of 'I'll have my bond' (III.3.4, 12 and 13) signifies mental disturbance and agitation. At the trial scene, he is completely unwilling to consider a more merciful course of action in his pursuit of justice.

- His friend and community elder, Tubal, has respect for Shylock, but even his daughter Jessica flees his household, calling it 'hell' (II.3.2). The audience may be torn between sympathy for Jessica and pity for Shylock who becomes increasingly solitary and surrounded by enemies.

PART FOUR, page 61

SECTION ONE: CHECK YOUR KNOWLEDGE

1 Ducats

2 Portia's father

3 Two of Portia's suitors

4 At the synagogue

5 Venice's commercial and financial centre (also the name of the area's famous bridge)

6 Bassanio, love and marriage

7 'mercy'

8 Lancelot Gobbo

9 Shylock

10 They are the destinations of Antonio's ships

SECTION TWO: CHECK YOUR UNDERSTANDING

- Bassanio and Portia's marriage is seen to be a loving one and the two characters are clearly attracted to each other. However, words like 'prize' and 'fortune' are a reminder that marriage is also a financial alliance and transaction between families.

- Portia is presented from the beginning of the play as wealthy and Bassanio describes her to Antonio in Act I Scene 1 as 'richly left'. We also learn in this scene of Bassanio's extravagances in the past, and understand that Bassanio's attempt to marry Portia is motivated at least partly by money. The husband to a wealthy heiress like Portia would receive a considerable dowry.

- The casket test symbolises the idea of marriage. Suitors make a choice but are also, in a sense, 'chosen', and the romantic and the monetary become intermingled.

- There are two other marriages in the play: between Nerissa and Gratiano, and between Lorenzo and Jessica. The trick with the rings that Nerissa and Portia play, and Lorenzo and Jessica's conversation at the start of Act V Scene I about classical lovers, remind the audience that while the play ends happily for these characters, marriage will be a lifelong test of loyalty.

PART FIVE, page 69

SECTION ONE: CHECK YOUR KNOWLEDGE

1. Act I Scene 2
2. Bassanio and Gratiano
3. Rhyming couplet
4. Words connected to death
5. 'poison'
6. Silent (like a mime artist), and a drunkard

7. Malapropism
8. Mood changes from excitement after his success in casket test to shock and anxiety on hearing about Antonio's problems
9. Words connected to the law
10. 'ring'

SECTION TWO: CHECK YOUR UNDERSTANDING

- The play is best described as a comedy, with its happy gathering of characters at the end, joined in friendship and marriage.

- The character of Shylock, an outsider throughout the play, becomes a threat to their happiness over the course of the play. This provides this comic play with its 'problem'. The problem reaches a climax in Act IV Scene 1 but is 'solved'.

- However, the character of Shylock is written with pathos and may elicit pity from audiences, particularly modern ones. The play was written in a context of intolerance towards Jews. Shakespeare's audiences are likely to have shared most Venetians' anti-Semitic attitudes, and viewed Shylock as a villain.

- The play contains much humour, from the visual humour and wordplay of the Gobbos, to the light-hearted tone of the play's Belmont scenes. However, Shakespeare is also exploring deeper and more serious themes in these scenes, such as prejudice, loyalty and the true value of things.

MARK SCHEME

POINTS YOU COULD HAVE MADE

- In the extract, Shylock despairs that his daughter has taken some of his money and jewels with her when she eloped with Lorenzo. Their wild spending (Act III Scene 1) may remind us of Bassanio's extravagance, referred to in Act I Scene 1.

- Solanio describes Shylock as 'confus'd' (line 12) because he seems to mourn the loss of his daughter ('My daughter!') and his money ('O my ducats!') equally and almost interchangeably (line 15). Solanio's description portrays Shylock as a stereotypically mean moneylender.

- Towards the end of this extract, there is the hint that one of Antonio's ships might be in difficulty. The ship was 'richly fraught' (line 31), an indication of the value of the goods the ship was carrying when it 'miscarried' (line 30).

- Antonio is the 'merchant' of the play's title. The play is set in Venice which was at the time a major centre for international trade. The play constantly reminds us of the insubstantial and risky nature of money, that it can be spent, stolen, given away or even lost at sea, all too easily.

- Shylock is a Jewish moneylender or usurer who charges interest on loans, unlike Christian lenders. The events in the play are set in motion by Bassanio's request for a loan from Antonio, and Shylock's unusual demand of a 'pound of flesh' (IV.1.230), means that the news of a lost ship in this scene creates anxiety and tension.

- Money also features in the play through inheritance. Portia is a wealthy heiress and must subject her suitors to a test to see who may marry her. The test features caskets with different monetary values – gold, silver and lead – but the value of their contents is at odds with this.

GENERAL SKILLS

Make a judgement about your level based on the points you made (above) and the skills you showed.

Level	Key elements	Spelling, punctuation and grammar	Tick your level
Very high	**Very well-structured answer which gives a rounded and convincing viewpoint.** You use very detailed analysis of the writer's methods and effects on the reader, using precise references which are fluently woven into what you say. You draw inferences, consider more than one perspective or angle, including the context where relevant, and make interpretations about the text as a whole.	You spell and punctuate with consistent accuracy, and use a very wide range of vocabulary and sentence structures to achieve effective control of meaning.	
Good to High	**A thoughtful, detailed response with well-chosen references.** At the top end, you address all aspects of the task in a clearly expressed way, and examine key aspects in detail. You are beginning to consider implications, explore alternative interpretations or ideas; at the top end, you do this fairly regularly and with some confidence.	You spell and punctuate with considerable accuracy, and use a considerable range of vocabulary and sentence structures to achieve general control of meaning.	
Mid	**A consistent response with clear understanding of the main ideas shown.** You use a range of references to support your ideas and your viewpoint is logical and easy to follow. Some evidence of commenting on writers' effects, though more needed.	You spell and punctuate with reasonable accuracy, and use a reasonable range of vocabulary and sentence structures.	
Lower	**Some relevant ideas but an inconsistent and rather simple response in places.** You show you have understood the task and you make some points to support what you say, but the evidence is not always well chosen. Your analysis is a bit basic and you do not comment in much detail on the writer's methods.	Your spelling and punctuation is inconsistent and your vocabulary and sentence structures are both limited. Some of these make your meaning unclear.	